WITHDRAWN

WITHDRAWN

THE TOWRE

# VILLAGE LONDON

# LONDON

## PAST & PRESENT

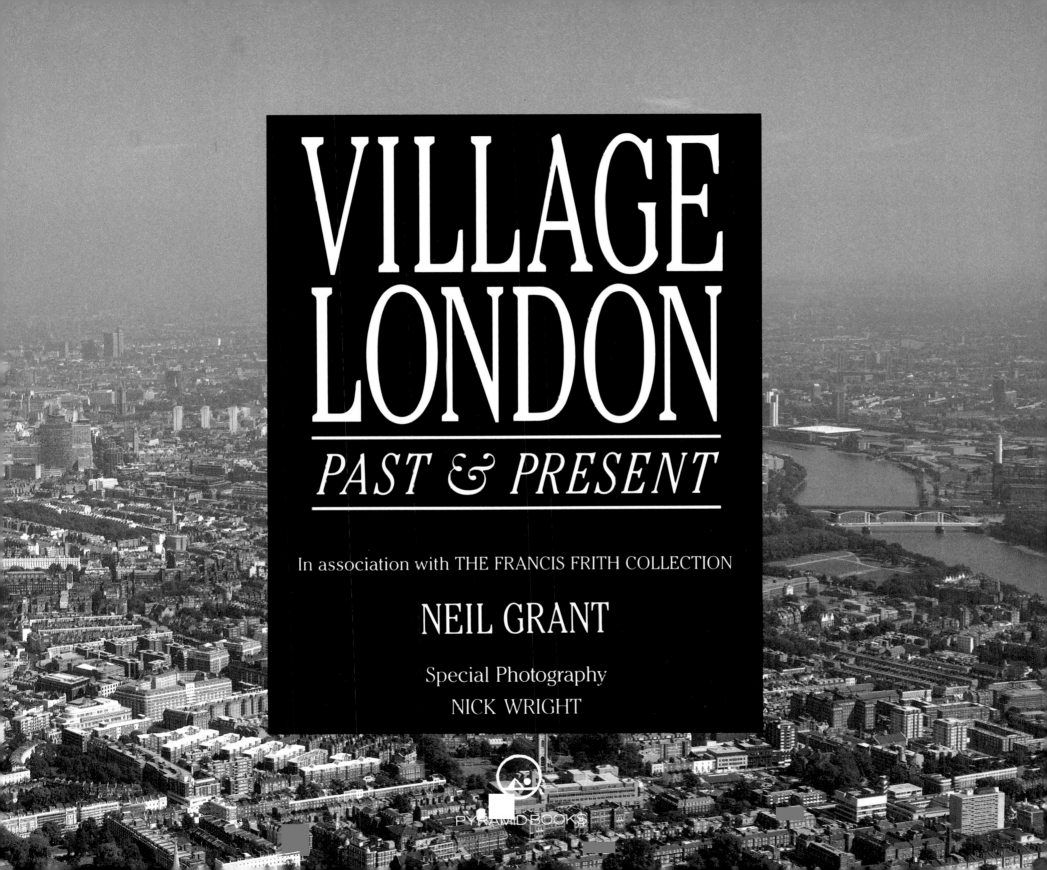

# VILLAGE LONDON

## PAST & PRESENT

In association with THE FRANCIS FRITH COLLECTION

### NEIL GRANT

Special Photography

NICK WRIGHT

PYRAMID BOOKS

PYRAMID BOOKS

**London Zoo** c. 1913

First published in 1990
by Pyramid Books, an imprint of
The Octopus Publishing Group plc
Michelin House, 81 Fulham Road
London SW3 6RB

© 1990 The Octopus Publishing Group plc

ISBN 1 871307 90 2

Produced by Mandarin Offset
Printed and bound in Hong Kong

# CONTENTS

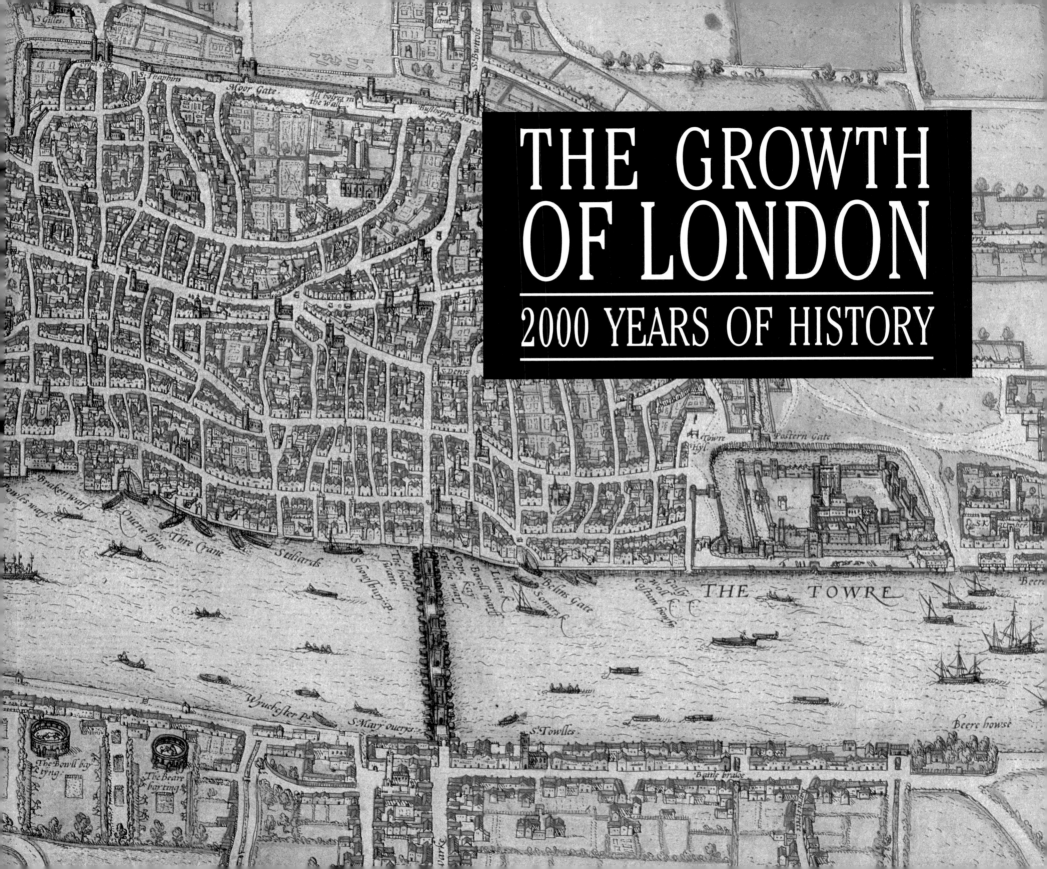

# THE GROWTH OF LONDON

## 2000 YEARS OF HISTORY

Although there were settlements in the area of what is now Greater London in prehistoric times (Stone Age tools have been found in Piccadilly), they were not of much significance. The physical conditions which were later responsible for London's extraordinary growth were, in pre-Roman times, rather a negative influence. Thus, the River Thames, London's main artery for many centuries, became so only after much work had been done to confine it to its course. Although the sea level was lower two thousand years ago, the Lower Thames spread itself liberally over the countryside at times of high tide or flood, and meandered for miles through swamps and marshes where no permanent settlement was possible. North of the Downs and east of the Chilterns, the well-drained chalk gave way to clogging London clay, not an infertile soil but hard to work even with iron tools. Much of the area was thickly wooded, and between the oak trees of the forest thrived an uninviting mass of brambly undergrowth. Property speculators would have shaken their heads over it.

Even the largest permanent settlements at that time in Britain hardly merited the name of town, but such as they were they were not to be found in the London area. It was only with the arrival of a truly urban people, the Romans, that the history of London really began.

## The Romans

The first Roman to cross the Thames was Julius Caesar, in relentless pursuit of the Belgae, the last wave of Celtic immigrés, who had reached Britain not long before. Exactly where Caesar crossed the river is uncertain – it was possibly some way upstream of the future city – and having made their presence felt, the Romans withdrew swiftly from the land of blue-painted barbarians, as Caesar libellously described the Ancient Brits.

During the century that followed, between Caesar's raids and the permanent invasion of AD 43, Britain was already becoming Romanized. The earliest genuine 'towns' can reasonably be dated to this period, though London was probably not among them. The largest town in the country then was Colchester, which was to be an important Roman city; however, within a very short time after the Roman conquest, Londinium (the Romans seem to have adopted the Celtic name) was on the map.

Then as now, London owed its existence largely to its convenience as a point of communications and transit. Like many another great city, it was sited at the point nearest the sea where the river could be crossed without undue difficulty. This depended not so much on the dimensions of the river itself as on the nature of its banks. At what is now Cornhill and Ludgate Hill, opposite Southwark on the south bank, well-drained land was to be found on both sides of the river. There the Romans built their fort and, in due course, a bridge, and there the city of Londinium developed.

Not without an early hiccup. The Iceni under their queen Boudicca (Boadicea), having sacked Roman Colchester in the temporary absence of the legions, descended on the embryonic wood-built city in AD 61 and virtually destroyed it. Burnt timbers have been found testifying to the depredation wrought by that early Iron Lady. However, the city was soon rebuilt, with defensive walls of stone and concrete up to 12 feet thick and 20 feet high to resist possible future invaders.

**London Wall** (right) The Roman city wall in the course of construction, 200 AD, as reconstructed and painted by Alan Sorell and displayed in the Museum of London.

**Heathrow** (left) Reconstruction of a Neolithic settlement found near Heathrow. The reconstruction, by Alan Sorell, is displayed in the Museum of London. The building in the foreground with a porch is a temple, and there were about a dozen huts. Archaeological excavation was rather hurried because the find was made during construction of London's main airport at Heathrow!

**London** Detail from a map of 1766. Apart from Kensington Palace, which was beginning to attract neighbours, the scene in Paddington, Earl's Court, Hammersmith and such places was predominantly of fields and small villages.

All roads converged on London, from the west as well as the north and south, and it became inevitably the chief commercial centre of the Roman province. Watling Street, running south-east to the Channel and north-west to St Albans and Chester, was the first. The roads were built not for merchants but for the military, although in the long run that was incidental. All roads, the Romans might say, led to Rome, but in Britain all roads led to London – as they continued to do, more or less, until that very situation compelled the construction of one that did not, the M25.

For some three centuries after Boudicca's revolt, London prospered under the *Pax Romana*, becoming one of the largest and wealthiest cities of the Empire outside Italy. By modern standards it was, of course, very small. The Roman walls, as they stood about the middle of the 2nd century, ran from a point on the river near the future Tower, via Aldgate and Bishopsgate to Cripplegate, then via Aldersgate and Newgate back to the river at Blackfriars. Rather surprisingly, the wall was continued along the river.

Though one of the most substantial of Roman provincial cities, Londinium was not one of the most elegant. Still, it contained some fine buildings. One of the most exciting of the many archaeological finds of recent years was the Temple of Mithras (a god much favoured by soldiers), including a remarkable head of the god, which was made, however, in Italy, not Britain. The remains of the Temple can now be seen in Bucklersbury House. A reconstruction in the light of the most recent knowledge of Londinium as a whole is to be seen in the London Museum in the Barbican.

In the 4th century Londinium was already in decline, the result of weakening administration and shrinking trade. Archaeological evidence shows that buildings ruined by fire in the late 4th century were not repaired, and after the final withdrawal of the legions in 410 Londinium rapidly became a ghost town. Probably it was still inhabited, but it was of little interest to the non-urban Germanic people who were arriving on southern coasts in growing numbers, while the virtually total loss of trade destroyed the city's chief *raison d'être*.

## The Saxons

Nevertheless, if the City of London is essentially a Roman foundation, the towns and villages that today make up Greater London owe much more to the Saxons than to the Romans. The Saxons were better able to cope with the unpropitious physical conditions of the area than their Celtic predecessors, and they naturally liked to make their settlements near river or sea. Most of the places, and in some cases the present names, of the London region were established two or three hundred years or more before the Norman Conquest. Essex takes its name from the kingdom of the East Saxons, similarly Middlesex from the Middle Saxons.

The circumstances which had made London the chief city of Roman Britain had not changed, and as the Germanic pagans gradually turned into God-fearing Englishmen the importance of London was reasserted. St Augustine may have chosen to make Canterbury his headquarters, but the bishopric of London was established within the next generation. By the 9th century the city was approaching the size and status it had held in Roman times, and many places in the Greater London area, such as Westminster or Barking, gained a new individuality as the location of major religious communities, glowing centres of civilization in the otherwise rather primitive society of the early Middle Ages.

## Norsemen and Normans

The Vikings disrupted these promising developments, sacking the abbeys and burning a good part of London (839). King Alfred stopped the rot, and in his treaty with Guthrum which divided England between Saxons and Danes, London was (rather narrowly) included in the Saxon part. Alfred rebuilt the defences, and in 894 a Danish raid up the River Lea was soundly trounced at Tottenham. In the 10th century London was practically the only town in England that could be considered safe against attack, and its position as the richest and most important city in the kingdom was fully restored. Until this time, however, the Saxons had built exclusively in wood, and visible traces of their city are therefore as scarce as those of the Romans.

After William the Conqueror had overcome the Saxon King Harold at the Battle of Hastings, there was no doubt about his immediate destination. The London magnates were not much inclined to dispute his claim of sovereignty and although it would be going too far to say they welcomed him with open arms, his arrival in London was a good deal more decorous than it might have been in more patriotic times. As a result, the City of London suffered no serious interruption of its march towards greater prosperity, and in spite of the authoritarian presence of William's White Tower the City magnates secured, and thereafter maintained, a considerable degree of independence from the Crown.

## The two cities

By 1066 the future capital was already, in effect, two cities – Westminster and the City itself, with easy communication by river but otherwise separated both by open space and by differing preoccupations. The City remained the centre of trade and finance, while around the rebuilt abbey on its island in the marshes of Westminster, a different sort of town was growing. It is too early to call it the seat of government, since the seat of government was the royal court and the royal court was then a highly peripatetic institution; but by the end of the Middle Ages, that was what it had become.

Medieval London was relatively wealthy but also insanitary and very crowded. Matters were not improved by the tendency of big City merchants to proclaim their importance by frequently rebuilding their houses on a grander scale and, later, by the palaces of lay and religious magnates which made such a show in the Strand in Stuart times.

**London Bridge**, painted in the middle of the 17th century by Claude de Jong. Today this picture may be seen in Kenwood House, Hampstead, among the magnificent collection which Lord Iveagh, the Guinness magnate, bequeathed to the nation in 1927.

The City's relations with the royal government were those of mutual dependence: wise monarchs did not alienate the merchants, at least not if they could help it. Trade was controlled by the guilds, the ancestors of the still-extant livery companies, and since they controlled trade they also controlled the City government. The Guildhall survives as a sign of the power of the medieval business community, though, grand as it was, it hardly compared with the vast and imposing multitude of religious buildings – abbeys, churches, 'hospitals', and so on – which were architecturally the dominant feature. There were over one hundred churches in the medieval City, of which hardly one complete example remains.

London was cosmopolitan and boisterous. The Jews were expelled in the 13th century, but there were various other groups of foreigners for Londoners to pick on, and the apprentices were always ready for a rough-and-tumble. More serious unrest, while eliciting plenty of support in London itself, tended to originate in Kent. Whether this was due to Jutish ancestry, the proponderance of heart-of-oak yeomen-farmers, or merely to the county's rougher weather, has not been decided.

Before the end of the 15th century London had spread well beyond its medieval walls, which roughly encompassed the traditional 'square mile' of the City. Southwark was a sizable town, rivalling the City in industrial crafts. Villages to the east, governed from the Tower (hence the present Tower Hamlets) were being drawn in, and although northward development was hindered by the marshes of Moorfields, Holborn had become attached and unbroken buildings reached as far as the Temple in the west.

## Rural environs

Apart from the City and Westminster, the whole of the Greater London region was, of course, completely rural. The nostalgic idea of London as a collection of villages is founded on the paradox that the settlements within twenty-odd miles of the City were, and long remained, more thoroughly rural than in almost any other region in the country, at least in the sense that they entirely lacked industry (except for simple country crafts). The fact that they were within comparatively easy reach of London, the chief industrial centre, naturally discouraged local industrial development. As elsewhere, life on the manor was largely self-sufficient, but what was not made at home could be obtained at the weekly market or the annual fair.

The rural character of London's environs had a 'ripple effect' over the centuries. The villages that we are concerned with here have long since become, first suburbs, then parts of the urban conglomeration; but there are still not many factories in the Home Counties.

Although a lot of land had been cleared – increasingly to feed the Londoners – much of Essex and Middlesex especially were still forested. 'Forest' does not necessarily mean thickly timbered, merely hunting country, yet it was said that to the north the woods, dark, forbidding and concealing bandits, were easily visible from the City walls. Queen Elizabeth I, when staying in Canonbury, found excellent hunting round about.

## Before the Fire

The 16th century in retrospect looks like a period of rapid progress and innovation – the modern age getting under way. The speed of change was certainly increasing, but many of the main social developments continued trends evident generations, even centuries, earlier.

The economic changes and commercial expansion of 16th-century England were most evident in London, whose inhabitants were at least more numerous than they had been before the Black Death (probably about 200,000 in the reign of Elizabeth). Except for the poorest class (and the unemployed were a growing problem) people generally were better off and, more important, more eager to be so. The dissolution of the monasteries and the execution of religious dissidents brought fortunes to Tudor yuppies and provided some eagerly exploited space in the congested City, where buildings were constantly being pulled down and rebuilt. A good many houses must have been sacrificed to make room for the opulent Elizabethan Royal Exchange.

Further signs of booming trade were the warehouses spreading along the south bank, which had also spawned, in the 'liberties' (outside City control), a recreational area (*Hamlet* or bear-baiting – both were popular).

New buildings were rising also in Westminster, notably the royal palace. Both there and in the City, however, all but the most wealthy men's houses were still built of wood, or wood and plaster, and with open fires and abundant rubbish, the place was a tinderbox.

Hollar's view of London in the reign of Charles I shows how it looked in the post-Elizabethan period. Very little of this city has survived: today one can get a better idea of London's appearance from old German towns.

Developments in London were repeated on a smaller scale in the small

**The Fire of London,** 1666, from a painting by an anonymous member of the Dutch school. The fire began in a baker's shop and in four days destroyed almost the whole of the medieval city, a disaster not without compensations, since much of what was destroyed was overdue for redevelopment.

towns round about, though rural districts suffered even more from the disappearance of the monasteries, not least in the deterioration of local services such as road maintenance and bridge building. The hiss of burning faggots in Mary's reign was heard in Uxbridge too, and the opulent Royal Exchange was repeated on a more modest scale in the form of many a new market house or guildhall, since the church porch no longer served the purpose. The link between commerce and the church was long commemorated by a market cross, such as that in Banbury to which one rode on a white horse. The Puritans swept away many of them, along with bishops and other objectionable relics of Rome.

## The march of time

Much more was to be swept away in the 17th century, an age of crisis and calamity, yet none of the great disasters of Civil War, plague, even the Great Fire, ultimately affected London's development so much as the less dramatic but more profound changes associated with the inevitable march of time, in particular the unstoppable flow of people from the country to the capital.

London had long since outgrown its medieval walls: by 1600 the City and Westminster were virtually one, though the buildings that linked them were mainly the spacious mansions of the mighty, more like country estates than town houses. London was still essentially the City as defined by the walls, which made up roughly half the developed area and far more than half the population. By 1700 this area had almost doubled and, in spite of laws against further building (the first 'green belt' policy – no more effective then than later), part of what became the West End had been laid out if not actually built.

One enormous improvement in Jacobean London was the construction in 1613 of the New River, which co-opted the source of the River Amwell in Hertfordshire to bring clean drinking water, by a canal 38 miles long, to the City, an epic of civil engineering. The scheme would not have been completed had not King James I purchased half the shares in the New River Company.

The City, almost solid for Parliament, was little affected by the Civil War,

**Custom House Quay,** 1757. The first custom house, to the east of the present site, was built in the 13th century. A later version went in the Great Fire, and this is Wren's replacement, which was itself burned down in 1814, at which time a larger building was already under construction next door.

though a line of forts was constructed around London, and completed by 1643. Westminster witnessed many of the main scenes of the drama, including the climax, the execution of the King outside the Whitehall Banqueting House built by Inigo Jones. Soldiers were quartered in the Abbey, where they ate off the altar and broke up the organ. The richly decorated Italian altar in Henry VII's chapel was dismantled and the 'painted images' destroyed. Fighting took place at many locations in the Greater London area, and at Brentford in 1642 the King shirked a battle and failed to seize the opportunity for an – admittedly hazardous – dash on the City, without possession of which his ultimate defeat was inevitable. At the end of the war the men of Kent, in traditional Kentish fashion, marched on London to demand peace, assembling according to time-honoured tradition on Blackheath, whence they were dispersed by General Fairfax without serious bloodshed.

During the Interregnum the march towards greater prosperity continued, with the merchants rubbing their hands over the capture of Jamaica (though they would have preferred Hispaniola). Puritanical influence caused the theatres to be closed and the prostitutes to be driven from the streets, but things soon reverted to normal when the monarchy was restored in 1660. Under the amused and cynical eye of Charles II, the merchants got on with their business of making money, while the King secretly obtained extra funds from the King of France.

### Disaster

Plague had made a comeback in London in the 17th century. The epidemic of 1625 was probably the worst since the Middle Ages, but the Great Plague of 1665 far exceeded it. At its peak in September, 7,000 deaths (perhaps an exaggeration) were recorded in a single day. It was worst, not surprisingly, in the most crowded districts.

The plague had not entirely disappeared when the Great Fire broke out in September 1666, spreading from a baker's shop in Pudding Lane to destroy, in the course of four days, almost the entire medieval City plus some districts outside the walls to the north and west. There were remarkably few deaths, but thousands were made homeless.

From our distant perspective, no longer much affected by individual tragedies, the Fire was in certain respects a blessing. For one thing, it put an end to the plague. That the disease never returned thereafter is probably due to other causes, possibly a change in the European rat population, but the Fire swept away many festering slums in which disease flourished. We may well regret the total loss of some fine buildings – Old St Paul's, the Royal Exchange, most of the halls of livery and 87 medieval churches – indeed almost the whole of Elizabethan London (the only substantial remnant survives in High Holborn). But without the Fire we should have been deprived of Wren's St Paul's; and Elizabethan London was doomed anyway. By 1666 it was already virtually impossible for large carts and carriages to negotiate the streets of the City; London would have ground to a halt long before without the great highway provided by the Thames.

The results of the Fire presented a fine opportunity for long-overdue replanning, but Wren's fine scheme for a new and spacious City was never carried out. The City fathers were in too much of a hurry to get on with business, and they balked at the costs. Nevertheless, Wren enjoyed more scope for his genius than falls to most great architects, and besides the sublime moment of the new cathedral, his masterpiece (and completed within his lifetime), he was responsible for about fifty new churches, some of whose endlessly imaginative spires grace the City today, despite the destruction wrought by the Blitz.

### The move westwards

The wooden City had gone. The new buildings were in brick and stone, less vulnerable to the awesome results of an ill-doused oven in a bakery.

The Fire also delivered an impetus to urban developments to the west, where aristocratic land speculators cashed in on the trend – apparent well before 1666 – for wealthy people to live farther from the centre. The Earl of Southampton built the first square in Bloomsbury; the Earl of St Albans was active in St James's; Nicholas Barbon and the Russell family (the Earl of Bedford had previously built residential Covent Garden, designed by Inigo Jones) around the Strand. The social centre of the capital, the world of wit and fashion, was no longer located in the City but farther west, nearer the Court.

By the end of the 17th century many small settlements were on the way to becoming suburbs, while remaining comparatively rural and non-industrial. Chelsea, for example, had terraced houses along the river as well as some large mansions like Beaufort House. Yet some 70 per cent of the area was given over to crops and pasture, and much of the remainder to parkland, gardens and common land. Actual buildings occupied a minute proportion. Kensington was still known chiefly as a supplier of fruit, vegetables and hay (a major commodity in pre-industrial cities), until William III, whose asthma was aggravated by the damp of Whitehall (or so he said), elected to live there, in spite of the likelihood of being cut off from Westminster whenever heavy rain made the roads impassable.

## The 18th Century

The burst of construction that followed the fire of London was exceptional, but London continued to grow throughout the 18th century, rapidly though unevenly, depending on such conditions as whether the British happened to be fighting the French or not (they often were). The process of growth, moreover, was not a simple one of steady outward expansion. While London continued to stretch outwards, other places within a few miles range of the capital were also expanding, until eventually they merged and became suburbs. Nor was progress equal in all directions. The main impulse was, as always, to the west, and development everywhere depended on transportation. Since there was only one bridge over the river until the first Westminster Bridge was built in 1728, expansion was confined mainly to the north bank. Farther out, towns and villages on the river tended to grow faster than places which were dependent for access to London on the deplorable roads, although from about 1760 roads began to improve.

The French wars, which slowed down construction, were nevertheless fought largely for the benefit of the City, as Britain extended its grasp on colonial trade. The Bank of England (founded 1694) symbolised the importance of commerce. For centuries the City held on to its old independence; at least it was no longer threatened with interference from royal government after the reign of Queen Anne. Its privileges were secure, its wealth (greater than ever) was safe too – and earning interest in the Bank.

Speculative building, though often realising large profits, was a risky business, producing bankrupts as well as millionaires. After the building boom of the late 17th century, things quietened down until after the Peace of Utrecht (1713), so that houses dating from the architecturally rewarding reign of Anne are unfortunately few. Some good examples that have survived can be seen in Queen Anne's Gate, formerly known as Queen Square.

Thereafter, the new housing of the West End, catering to the comfortably off rather than the digustingly rich, was considerably less spectacular. The modesty and conformity, doorways apart, of the residential streets and squares of Georgian London are considered one of the most attractive features of the capital as it is today. But they had to wait a long time to win this admiration. Nobody thought much of them until 20th-century developers started to pull them down. Some of the characteristics of these houses were the result of fire precautions. Brick was thus the almost universal material, and windows were deliberately recessed to reduce the amount of exposed, and inflammable woodwork. Only the doors were allowed a decorative flourish, although, once one passed through the door, one found oneself in rooms of considerable elegance as well as comfort.

## The West End

The West End took its more or less final shape in the 18th century. Again, the main developments were originated by aristocratic speculators, but they aimed at some fairly grand effects and employed the best architects. William Kent, who designed Horse Guards, laid out the gardens in Grosvenor Square. James Gibb designed several fine neoclassical churches, including St Mary-le-Strand and St Martin-in-the-Fields. The famous Hawksmoor-Vanbrugh combination, or more particularly the first half of it, was responsible for St Mary Woolnoth and others. Since Wren, if not since Inigo Jones, architecture had become a serious profession, and later in the century men like Adams and William Chambers (Somerset House) and Henry Holland ('Hans Town' and Sloane Street) commanded high respect.

Developments also took place in other areas, though more patchily. Bloomsbury and Fitzrovia were prime districts; George Dance, architect of the Mansion House, also designed Finsbury Square in 1777, which was the first place in London to have gas lighting installed (1807). Camden and Somerstown were developed, unlike most of the West End, as separate communities – 18th-century 'new towns' in fact. Islington, Shoreditch, Hoxton and Hackney became popular suburbs, surrounded by open country.

Development farther afield was often restricted by poor communications and, consequently, insecurity. City gents resident in Islington crossed the fields to work in groups with armed guards. However, Kensington and Hampstead were growing fast, and so were villages at a greater distance along the river. Twickenham, residence of Alexander Pope and Horace Walpole, was one of the most fashionable. South of the river City commuters took up residence in Dulwich, Camberwell and Greenwich. In general, Surrey and Kent developed faster with the construction of more bridges across the Thames.

In spite of high crime rates, London life was becoming less turbulent. The only serious popular disturbance was the so-called Gordon Riots of 1780, ostensibly anti-Catholic but reflecting other resentments too. On the whole, London was developing peacefully and steadily during the late 18th century, and this picture was not immediately disrupted by the vast upheavals, political and economic, which were eventually to change life drastically.

**Horse Guards Parade** in the 18th century, by John Chapman. It was originally the tilting yard of Whitehall Palace, scene of a famous tournament in the days of Henry VIII. The present building, constructed in the early 1750s, was designed by William Kent.

## Regency London

The growth of Britain's trade in the 18th century required expansion of the port facilities of London: the West India Docks were opened in 1802, the London Docks in 1805. The Grand Junction Canal and other waterways vastly improved internal freight transport, though the useful life of the canal system was to be a short one, regrettably perhaps.

In spite of the restrictions of wartime, some construction continued in other parts besides the docks. Sir John Soane's Bank of England, not to mention his Dulwich Art Gallery, were not aborted by Napoleon's threatened invasion, and Rennie's Waterloo Bridge was the most famous of three London bridges designed by that able engineer in the early years of the century. The relatively sudden profusion of Thames bridges opened up the Surrey bank to the builders when, after Napoleon was finally disposed of in 1815, speculative building again moved into high gear.

The great figure of the Regency period, so far as the development of London was concerned, was John Nash, who is remembered above all for the grand, shining facades to be seen in Regent's Park (the buildings behind them have been totally reconstructed), though he was responsible for far more than that, and he could turn his hand to Gothic castles – or thatched cottages for that matter – as easily as to his more familiar classical style. His great Regent's Park/Regent Street scheme was not carried out in every detail and, more's the pity, was rather rapidly replaced. At the end of his career Nash fell out of favour, was sacked from the Board of Works, and his plan for remodelling Buckingham Palace abandoned. Shame!

By the early 19th century great houses for great men had become much less common, though a few were still built, such as Apsley House, the Duke of Wellington's *pied à terre* in Town. To some extent great public buildings took the place of great private ones. The National Gallery and the British Museum are outstanding examples dating from the pre-Victorian period.

**Whitehall and the Privy Garden,** by Canaletto, (left) *c.* 1750. Richmond House is on the extreme right, next to Montagu House, with St Paul's and the Thames visible between them. At the end of the Privy Garden is the Banqueting Hall, with the Holbein Gate (demolished a few years later) opposite.

**Greenwich** A hokey-pokey stall in 1884 (right). Hokey-pokey was a form of cheap ice cream, a certain mystery surrounding its ingredients, and it was sold from barrows like this until the 1920s. The name is said to derive from 'hocus pocus', an expression used by conjurors as early as the 17th century.

## Social divisions

One feature of London which became firmly established in this period was the social divide between east and west. Merchants and bankers were no longer attracted to Stepney or Hackney and nor, therefore, were speculative builders. Some districts were showing symptoms of developing (if that's the right word) into the notorious slums of the Victorian East End, although Bethnal Green, where houses for the workers (chiefly weavers) were built, had not yet lost its attraction as a place for Sunday picnics.

The weavers' houses were a sign of the times. Yet the Industrial Revolution, under way in the 1780s, had comparatively little effect on London and the London region before the accession of Queen Victoria (1837). In the North, huge transformations had taken place: Lancashire mills had been grinding away for two generations; smallish ports and market towns had become teeming cities. But in the Southeast the effects were far less obvious. Machines had replaced human labour in towns and fields; new industries had started in many towns, though hardly on a Mancunian scale, and the accelerating drift of people from field to factory had caused unemployment problems in some places. Industrial slums were relatively small, isolated and easily ignored (as they still are), but London retained its ancient role – never discarded – of great *commercial* capital rather than industrial city. As some would say, though not quite fairly, the North had the muck, the brass stayed in town.

## Railways

The greatest changes to London – virtually the creation of Greater London as we know it – were the result of the second phase of the Industrial Revolution, in which progress was led by the railways.

Increasingly, since the early 18th century, people had used roads rather than the river, creating the frightful congestion on which many contemporaries remarked. Though more versatile than boats, carriages were no faster, and in central London coachmen practically had to force a way through the crowded streets. Still, carriage folk could afford to live some miles from town, while most lower-middle-class people – the vast army of clerks, for instance, who staffed the City offices – could not. They had to live more centrally, where the laws of supply and demand kept rents very high, and even thoroughly 'respectable' families could afford only a couple of rooms.

The railways changed all that. Quite suddenly it was possible to travel deep into the Kent countryside in greater comfort, at little cost and in hardly more time than it took to get from Clerkenwell to the City. This was the chief cause for the unparalleled expansion of London in the second half of the 19th century.

## Victorian expansion

The opportunities for speculative building were vast. Competition was fierce, it was still a risky business, but demand was enormous. It was, of course, a different sort of building, since the customers were considerably more numerous and less wealthy. Hence a certain lack of variety. Rows of houses went up which were not only identical to each other (even that was something of a novelty), but identical to the houses in the next street or, indeed, the next town.

The leapfrogging process with which we are more familiar today also applied: when the well-to-do found their semirural retreats being turned into suburbs and their employees becoming their neighbours, they simply moved on – farther out. The railways enabled them to reach the City or the West End in less time than they had taken before, when the distance was shorter, and they travelled First Class. Punctuality, itself a fairly recent concept, was in any case more important for employees than bosses.

The epidemic of bricks and mortar spread inexorably outwards. Many people deplored it, but none could stop it, which is more or less the situation a century later. Hundreds of rural villages became, in fifty years, crowded suburbs. The process can be measured in different ways, for instance by population statistics. The popular new residential areas recorded phenomenal leaps: Islington from 10,000 to 335,000 between 1800 and 1900, Hammersmith from 25,000 to 150,000 between 1850 and 1900.

Another indication is the increase in churches. The Victorian era was the greatest church-building period since the Middle Ages, growing population being combined with growing piety. Ealing had one parish church in 1850; by 1910 it had ten. Nonconformist chapels were going up equally fast. As their congregations generally had less money, most were undistinguished buildings, to say the least, but taken as a group, the neo-Gothic Anglican churches of the Victorian era are not very inspirational either.

**King's Cross Station,** *c.* 1870 and as it is today. The great railway termini offered new opportunities to architects. King's Cross station is remarkably functional, notwithstanding its vaguely Venetian arches and clock tower, and might have been built eighty years later than it was (1852). It was the work of Lewis Cubitt, brother of the developer of Belgravia, and was built on the site of an old hospital.

The problems involved in providing the capital with a national railway service were enormous. Inevitably, thousands of people were made homeless (and the compensation was often inadequate). Even so, the railway lines could not be brought into the very centre as this would have entailed the demolition of half the capital.

Railways naturally encouraged the growth of those places which happened to lie along the route they followed. There, speculative builders erected rows of 'Railway Villas', 'Railway Cottages', etc., names then redolent of the romance of progress though later they acquired a different connotation. When the trains arrived, the population shot up in an extraordinary way. For example, the population in Walthamstow in about 1870, just before completion of the Chingford line, was only about 10,000; by 1900 it was close to 100,000.

Other villages which looked ripe for expansion failed to do so because the railway passed them by. Bromley and Ruislip were two such places, temporarily outgrown by lesser neighbours with a more convenient railway station. Kingston was another, although there the absence of a railway station in the town resulted from the resistance of the townspeople, who did not want the beastly thing. Neighbouring Surbiton, an insignificant village, got the railway instead, and within a few years Surbiton was the equal, in terms of population, of Kingston.

## Industry

The march of bricks and mortar continued over land used previously for agriculture which, until the late 18th century, was far the most important economic activity outside central London. Although there were still dairy cows in Islington in about 1900, this loss of agricultural land plus the rise in population meant that corn and hay, fruit and vegetables, had to come from farther afield, a prime cause for improvements in transportation. The Grand Junction Canal brought produce from the Midlands. Canals, railways and improved roads made London the market for a very large region (hence, too, the rise of Covent Garden).

Industries generally developed along the Thames and its tributaries, which provided both transportation and power, until steam became universal. At the beginning of the 19th century there were some forty mills on the River Wandle alone, many of them flour mills but others engaged in a variety of activities, from gunmaking to printing. Brewing and brick-making were established industries almost everywhere in the 18th century, and among other common traditional industries were cloth-bleaching, wax-making and quarrying.

Fishing was as old as farming. Billingsgate market existed in Norman times, and until well into the 19th century fishing was an important occupation in ports with easy access to the sea, like Barking, but also in little river towns like Teddington. The Thames was once a famous salmon river, but canalisation and pollution put an end to that. An average of 32

salmon a year were taken at Boulter's Lock in the decade 1795-1804; in the decade 1812-21 the average was eight; after 1824 it was nil. (Recently attempts, possibly misguided, have been made to reintroduce the Atlantic salmon to the Thames.) The case of the Lea was even worse. Still an excellent angling river around 1850, fish were practically eliminated by industry and the Lea Navigation scheme. By that time steamships and railways had made it feasible to import fresh fish from a much greater distance, and the British had already lost their taste for freshwater fish. Fishing as a full-time occupation virtually ceased; the Barking fleet moved to Great Yarmouth.

In the City industry was forced out by business, and tended to concentrate beyond the old walls to the east. Traditional industries like pottery, glass, furniture and leatherwork thrived especially in Southwark, 'the City's workshop'. But every community was affected in one way or another by industrial growth. On the whole, it was not a matter of new products so much as a total change in methods. Factories, machines, steam power, high capitalization, division of labour, the shift system – it was a different world.

## Breathing spaces

In spite of the unceasing expansion of London, every visitor to the capital remarks on the extraordinary quantity of open space and greenery. In some respects this is a happy accident, for in the early 19th century it was common for progressive persons to remark deprecatingly on surviving unbuilt-up spaces. 'What a waste!' was a common reaction. Nevertheless, the common people were, and long had been, intent to preserve their 'commons' or 'fields' against the incursions of landlords. The battle against enclosure was a constant theme of English history from the 16th century.

Eighteenth-century building schemes were often arranged around a square which was filled with gardens. Many of them have survived, even when the buildings around them have not, and although some are not open to the public they at least offer a prospect of trees and flowers instead of bricks and concrete. They largely account for the openness of London outside the City.

Larger areas – the big parks – are often the result of the immense royal hunting preserves. Some, like Hyde Park, were once ecclesiastical property

**Erith** Fraser and Chalmers foundry about 1907. The company made machinery for the South African gold mines. Labour was intensive in those days, and a 54-hour working week was still common.

which passed to the Crown during the Reformation. King Charles I and at least some later monarchs were surprisingly liberal in their attitude to public access, and once public access had been allowed it soon became 'customary' and therefore difficult to rescind. Attempts to exclude or limit the people using the parks were in any case difficult to enforce.

In the outer suburbs too, many of the large parks exist because they were formerly reserved for the king and his cronies. Richmond Park was a royal deer park; nearby Bushy Park was once part of the enormous Hampton Court Gardens, themselves now also open to the public.

Long before the end of the 19th century the desirability of keeping open spaces for recreation was generally recognised. Hampstead Heath and Epping Forest were deliberately secured for the benefit of London's citizens. There, as elsewhere, it was necessary to fight long and hard to retain 'common land' on the fragile basis of 'custom'. Thus was Wimbledon Common, with its windmill, preserved from the planned developments of Lord Spencer, and the act of 1886 banning the enclosure of common land within 14 miles of Charing Cross was a great help.

The preservation of space and greenery became all the more desirable as they became more scarce, and in the 1930s resulted in the Green Belt scheme to encircle London in a swathe of mainly agricultural land. The Green Belt survives, yet Greater London has continued to spread beyond it.

**The Houses of Parliament,** c. 1870 (inset) and today. After the mediaeval Palace of Westminster was burned down in 1834, nearly one hundred plans were submitted for the new palace, and those of Charles Barry were selected. A condition of the competition was that the building should be in the English Gothic style, and Barry, more of a classicist by instinct, called in that genius of the Gothic Revival, Augustus Pugin. Barry provided the plan, Pugin the ornamentation (right down to the inkwells) and they proved a remarkable team. The result was greeted with almost universal approval from that day to this. Building began in 1837 and the House of Commons was ready for use within ten years. The clock tower, now known as Big Ben though that was originally the name given to the bell, was finished ten years later, after many bitter arguments and technical problems with both clock and bell.

The palace was finished in 1860, and the inset photograph was taken not many years later, before the creation of Victoria Tower Gardens. That green oasis, with Rodin's Burghers of Calais, now fills the area which is here still occupied by flour mills, wharves, cranes, coal barges and lighters. Just south of this spot, quail could be shot in the early 19th century, and the Millbank prison still covered the future site of the Tate Gallery (1897).

## Victorian City

During the reign of Queen Victoria the population of Greater London increased at a rate which approached an average of 25 per cent per decade. In central London the rise was naturally less startling, and in the City itself the population was in decline. This process, sometimes spoken of as if it were a 20th-century phenomenon, had been going on since the 17th century. In 1801 the population of the City was about 120,000, less than half of what it had been at the Restoration; by 1901 it had fallen to 26,000 and it continued to shrink in the 20th century (by 1951 it was down to 5,000). The main reason is obvious. The demand for office space could only be met by the destruction of housing, and for good or ill many pleasant Georgian residential districts were swept away, to be replaced by often splendid, if sometimes florid, Victorian office blocks, which in our own time have been giving way to the glass, steel and concrete towers of the modern city.

Yet, paradoxically, just beyond the boundaries of the City, lay the worst slums in London, with such great numbers crushed into such a small area that it is hard to imagine how they all found room to lie down at night.

One fine old tradition of medieval London came to its long-delayed end when the last and greatest of the annual 'fairs', St Bartholomew's, was wound up in 1840, the shops and stores of the West End having made it redundant. On the other hand, the great wholesale markets flourished as never before. Smithfield (which, however, ceased to deal in live cattle in 1855) and Billingsgate were long established; Covent Garden, long the traditional resort of flower sellers, became the chief fruit and vegetable market in 1833. The docks continued to expand: the Victoria Dock opened in 1855, Millwall Dock in 1868, the Royal Albert in 1880.

To a great extent central London was rebuilt during the 19th century. An hour's stroll around the capital today demonstrates that, hardly less than Manchester or Glasgow, London is essentially a Victorian city. While we may regret much that was lost then, it cannot be denied that by the end of the century London was more spacious, more convenient and much less insanitary than it had been two or three generations earlier, and it had assumed a form which remained largely unchanged until the 1940s.

Some of the rebuilding was enforced by circumstances. Trafalgar Square, originally conceived by Nash, was created against strong opposition and replaced what had become a very scruffy district, but the greatest single building complex of the age resulted from an accident. The old Palace of Westminster, except for the Great Hall, was destroyed by fire in 1834. It was rebuilt in sixteen years in that remarkable mixture of styles which like many, though by no means all, examples of Victorian eclecticism, resulted in a proud, graceful, harmonious whole (even allowing for the effect of familiarity in creating a sense of homogeneity). The new clock tower superseded the Tower as the most popular symbol of London.

## Traffic

In spite of a general increase in space, central London was faced with traffic problems even worse than today's. Holborn Viaduct, the Highgate Archway scheme (a saga of disaster until the great Telford got his hands on it), Blackwall Tunnel, the Embankment, indeed the major road layout much as it exists today, represent the efforts made to ease the flow of traffic in 19th-century London.

A perennial problem was the lack of a central planning authority (a requirement, so far as traffic is concerned, no less evident today). This was not achieved until the Metropolitan Board of Works was set up in 1855, followed by the London County Council in 1888. The metropolitan boroughs were created in 1900 and lasted until the reorganization of local government which came into effect in 1965. County Hall, the imposing headquarters first of the LCC and then of the GLC, occupies a commanding site on the south side of the river and is still one of the most distinctive buildings in London. A public competition was held for the design of the building and the winner was a young architect Ralph Knott – one of the unsuccessful competitors was the much better known architect Edwin Lutyens.

Building the terminuses for the main railway lines was in itself a huge undertaking (Euston, opened in 1838, was the first), but central London in particular remained dependent on the horse-drawn omnibus (steam-driven omnibuses plied between Paddington and the City and on a few other routes for a while in the 1830s) and the hackney cab. The problem was not to get from a distant suburb into town, but to get from the railway station to the office. Progressive planners, in particular a solicitor named Charles Pearson, suggested an underground railway. The idea met terrific opposition, but so had the surface railways, by which means, the elderly Duke of Wellington had warned, a French army might arrive in the capital before the news of its landing. (Similar arguments were advanced against a Channel Tunnel a century later.) But the chief objection was that underground tunnels would make buildings unsafe. Many years passed before Parliament could be persuaded to countenance a line to connect the main northern terminuses, a good many more before the requisite financing could be arranged. At last, Mr Gladstone was able to travel on the North Metropolitan Line, from Paddington to Farringdon Street (nearly four miles) in 1862. No buildings had collapsed – in fact the line, built by the 'cut and cover' technique, passed under few. The technique consisted of digging a trench, walling the sides and laying the track, then roofing it over and restoring the road surface above (the track usually ran below a road to avoid having to pay for expensive property). Although it was rather smoky (the railway was steam operated, so was inevitably somewhat grimy), the enterprise was an immediate success, carrying almost ten million passenger in its first year. The line was soon extended, and was followed by the building of the District and Circle lines, also by the 'cut and cover' method. The first real 'tube', with electric trains, running from the Bank under the Thames via Waterloo to Stockwell, opened in 1890.

***Turnpike Lane*** *1932*

**Charing Cross** in the 1890s. The original cross which marked the last resting place of the funeral procession of Queen Eleanor in 1290 mouldered away in the 17th century. The remains were used to pave Whitehall. The present cross in the station forecourt, which is alleged to be a replica of the original, was erected in 1865.

## The 20th Century

In the 20th century London has been remade again. It has grown ever larger and, measured by people and buildings rather than by official boundaries, it is now close to occupying the whole southeastern quarter of England. It has changed too, not out of all recognition, yet the London of today is as different from the London of 1900 as the London of 1900 was from that of the Regency.

The influences bringing about social change were not confined to London but, as in earlier periods, reflected national or even international trends. Among the factors which most obviously affected the growth and appearance of Greater London was progress towards a more egalitarian society, in particular the increasing prosperity of what may be called the lower middle class, and the rising influence, both in the home and public life, of women.

A second powerful influence was the internal combustion engine. The effect of motor cars and buses on mobility was as great, eventually greater, than that of the railways. Motor vehicles could go wherever there were roads, and roads, most of them admittedly in need of improvement, opened up a much greater area than the limited railway lines. In the outer suburbs it was no longer necessary to live within easy reach of the station.

It is interesting to trace the effect on suburban development of changes in transportation during the past two hundred years. Suppose Town A is on the main road to London twenty or thirty miles away. In the early 19th century, when stagecoach travel is at its peak, Town A prospers. When the railway is built, though, it avoids Town A and passes through Town B, its sleepy neighbour several miles east or west. Now Town B develops rapidly, and Town A becomes the sleepy neighbour. But in the early 20th century, motor vehicles restore the importance of the roads, and Town A rises again. To stretch the argument perhaps further than it will reasonably go, Town A may miss out again in the 1980s when the junctions of the motorway are inconveniently placed!

Motor vehicles also encouraged the building of new roads, accompanied by 'ribbon development', and the tentacles of the great octopus were able to reach into hitherto untouched parts by extension of the Underground to places such as Cockfosters, at the end of the Piccadilly Line.

## Between the wars

The housing boom that took place between the two world wars was the biggest yet, in spite of postwar slump, General Strike and Great Depression. Unbridled speculation and fast-rising property prices characterised a period in which planning was virtually nonexistent, although by the 1930s the situation had improved somewhat in this respect. It was, however, only the Depression that saved the Green Belt.

The bulk of the new housing was for people of modest means. It was the era of the semi. Practically the whole of what remained available in Middlesex disappeared under a sea of unpretentious, vaguely traditional houses, three- or four-bedroomed 'villas', sometimes displaying modest awareness of Art Deco with a little coloured glass in the porch. And not only Middlesex; the great red tide (tiled roofs were in) flowed all around, covering the last of the agricultural land within twenty miles of London. They were not bad houses; most are still in good condition now, but they were not very interesting and they were all, more or less, *the same*!

A large proportion of new residential construction was municipal housing. This was also the era of the council estate, and in Dagenham the L.C.C. built, on land specially purchased, what was said to be the largest housing estate in the world. Teething problems were severe, but in the end the Becontree estate turned out to be a much greater success than many of the schemes for rehousing East Enders after 1945.

Housing schemes for the better-off were fewer and smaller, the most notable example being the pre-1914 Hampstead Garden Suburb, and in the inner boroughs a large and growing proportion of residents lived in flats.

In central London the West End changed more than the City. The last slums were cleared from the area of St Giles, and the last traces of Nash's buildings disappeared from Regent Street. Large new office blocks and shops arose, in a variety of styles ranging from traditional (a disillusioned modernist enquired whether Selfridges was intended to be a store or a Greek temple) to modern, like Peter Jones on Sloane Square or – perhaps the most advanced building of the thirties – Finsbury Health Centre, or – a London landmark rivalling St Paul's and Big Ben – Battersea Power Station. Among architectural oddities the most notable was Westminster Cathedral, not a negligible building in its own right but totally at odds with its environment.

Remaining big houses were disappearing or changing roles, most happily as hotels. Dorchester House became the Dorchester Hotel, joining Edwardian giants like the Ritz. Cinemas, replacing Victorian music halls, offered a new kind of opportunity to architects, and the results, though sometimes verging on the grotesque, did bring a touch of exoticism and fantasy into mundane lives, along with Hollywood films.

Commercial development, which had gradually depopulated the City over many years, was having the same effect on inner boroughs such as Southwark, Westminster, Hackney, even as far as Fulham. Slum clearance usually meant that people were rehoused farther out, an effect accelerated by the building of new streets such as the Kingsway-Aldwych thoroughfare between Holborn and the Strand, which was punched through a solid mass of buildings in 1905, and the 'clearance' effected by German bombs during the Blitz.

The corollary was, naturally, that other suburbs expanded. Prosperous Kensington and Hampstead increased steadily while more distant suburbs, like Hendon or Bexley, doubled and sometimes redoubled their population between the 1920s and the 1960s.

## World War II

During the Second World War nearly 30,000 people in London were killed by bombs and missiles, and some 50,000 were injured. As in all disasters, statistics leave us cold; the total human misery inflicted cannot be calculated so easily.

Large areas of London were almost completely flattened. In the City scarcely a building escaped fatal damage between Cheapside and the Barbican, or in the area between Southwark and London bridges and the Mansion House. North and east of St Paul's, large areas were equally devastated, but Wren's great church stood proudly (though not undamaged) amid the ruins, a bloomin' miracle, as people said. His smaller churches were less fortunate. Virtually every one of the sixteen standing in 1939 was a ruin (ten of them in one night) but – another minor miracle – most of the spires stayed upright, and nearly all Wren's churches have been successfully restored. The halls of the livery companies, mostly little known to the public, were other notable casualties, only two escaping more or less undamaged. Though buildings could be and have been restored, the paintings, manuscripts, art objects and, in the case of the livery halls, the marvellous Restoration woodwork they contained, were gone for ever.

If it is possible to think in such terms, there were compensations. Opportunities for replanning and rebuilding in more appropriate ways were presented (though not always accepted), and the archaeologists had a field

**St Paul's,** 1940. The survival of St Paul's during the Blitz was regarded as a miracle, as in one night alone 28 bombs fell around the building, but it was protected from damage by its own firewatchers, St Paul's Watch. The high explosive bombs which fell in the cathedral precincts were defused before they could go off, but the cathedral did not escape unscathed. This was the scene on 10 October 1940 after a bomb struck the east end, bringing masonry crashing down on the High Altar.

day. Without the destruction caused during the war, our knowledge of Roman and medieval London would be much poorer.

The years immediately after the war were austere indeed; only the willowherb flourished among the ruins. The first priority was to rehouse the homeless; less essential building had to be postponed, and even housing projects proceeded slowly.

## Postwar renewal

The period of renewal can conveniently be dated from the Festival of Britain (1951), a serendipitous though not initially popular project rather surprisingly promoted by a government in which the leading figure had been Mr Austerity himself, Sir Stafford Cripps.

After that the building boom was under way again and the face of London was again remade. The City, almost 90 percent rebuilt between 1950 and 1990, rose from the rubble, and 'rose' is certainly the word, in steel (actually the first steel-framed building was the Ritz in 1905), concrete and glass. The working classes, if they could not be persuaded to move to, say, Thetford, were rehoused in tower blocks, which proved to be unpopular, unsightly and, in the case of Ronan Point at least, unsafe.

There were other scandals, like the Centre Point building which stood empty long after its construction, apparently serving as a convenient tax loss, or the scurvy activities of slum landlords before the Rent Act provided greater protection for tenants. There were some fine modern buildings among the skyscrapers (Millbank Tower, the quixotic Post Office Tower) and other buildings, and some unappealing ones (the National Theatre). The Barbican scheme aimed to attract well-off residents back to the City, and the Docklands Development scheme, following the example of the earlier Thamesmead development, did the same for the docks, badly damaged during the war and doing much less business anyway.

## Social trends

These projects notwithstanding, London had become a place for working, no longer a place for living. The capital, nostalgically known as London Town, was no town; it was – lovely word – a conurbation. The population continued to grow, and the people continued to move outwards in search of

**The Festival of Britain** was held in 1951 on the south side of the Thames. The Royal Festival Hall, beyond the 'Skylon' obelisk, was the first of the buildings that now form the celebrated cultural complex on the site.

more pleasant, sometimes less expensive, environments. Some inner boroughs recovered in terms of population but declined in terms of living standards. A few areas, with high unemployment and soaring, drugs-related crime, descended to conditions arguably worse than the hideous Victorian slums pictured by Mayhew or Arthur Morrison. The Brixton riots and the lynching of a policeman at Broadwater Farm were the newsworthy signs of a desperate society.

The creation of the Greater London Council (replacing the L.C.C.) as a body more concerned with overall policy and co-ordination between local authorities failed to solve London's centuries-old problem: the lack of central planning. Property speculators encountered rising opposition, especially from 'green' groups, but money still carried more clout than culture. Conservationists, lent unexpected support by the Prince of Wales, registered some victories, but some fine old London landmarks disappeared nonetheless. There was an outcry over the destruction of the Euston Arch, a 72 ft high portico with huge Doric columns, built in 1838 to celebrate the completion of the London and Birmingham Railway.

Nothing, it seems, can be done about London's growth, which today encompasses not only the 600 square miles of Greater London but practically the whole of southeast England. London has always been the vortex, sucking in money and people from the rest of the country, and the affluence of the 1980s has exacerbated old problems: rocketing property values, largely due to a housing shortage, with home owners in the more spacious areas eagerly selling off their gardens to build a compact terrace of town houses; and desperate traffic congestion, so that a Porsche moves through central London more slowly than a one-horse hackney cab and an accident on, say, the M4 in Wiltshire threatens to bring traffic throughout Greater London to a standstill.

It is unlikely that these problems will be solved by mere mortals. If the worst comes to the worst they will, in some way or other, solve themselves, temporarily at least, as they have in the past. (A big fat slump would reduce building pressures besides thinning out the BMWs.) Clearly, there will have to be massive improvements in public transport as the oil runs out – though preferably earlier. Possibly the combination of high prices and deteriorating environment will make the Southeast relatively less attractive, and if not, many of us will have to learn to live in rather different conditions. In this book we look at the way London's 'villages' have changed during the past century. Although we may be surprised to find here and there how small the changes have been, the general transformation in our way of life has been enormous – and quite unforeseeable.

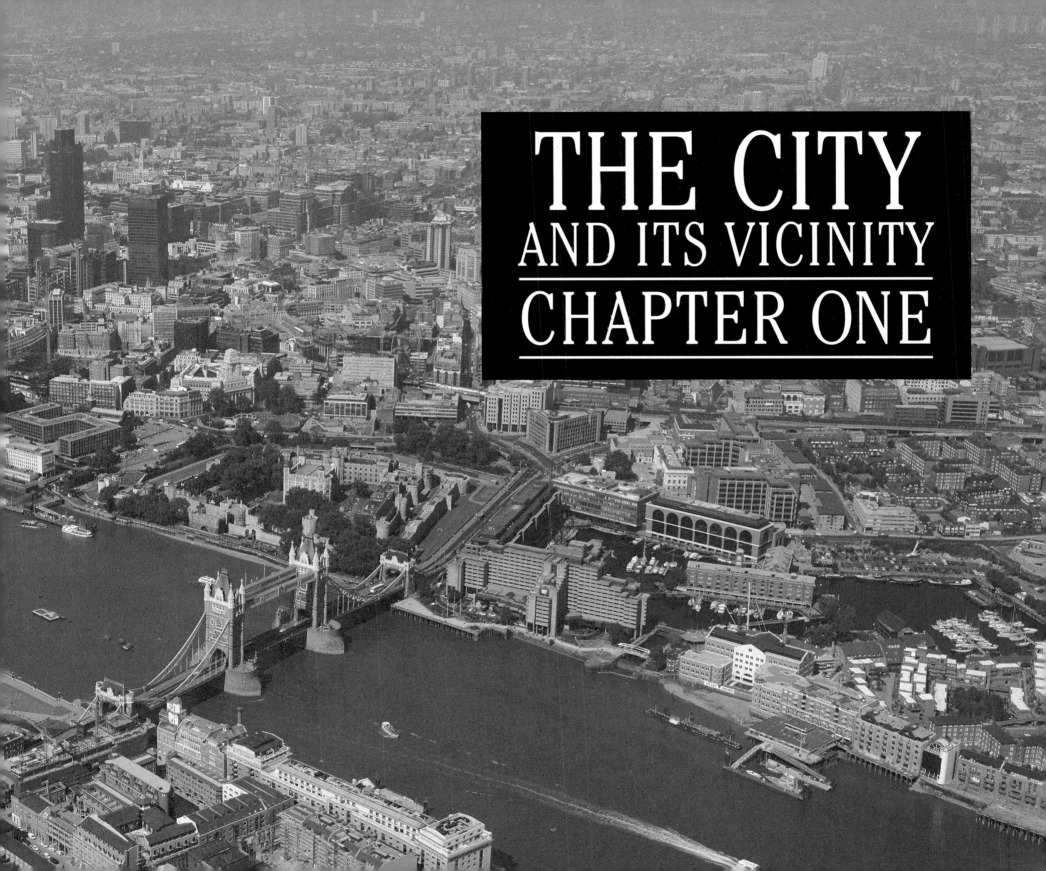

# THE CITY
## AND ITS VICINITY
## CHAPTER ONE

The traditional square mile of the city is a place full of historical paradox. Once upon a time the City *was* London, and to this day there is a residual feeling that it is the true heart and soul, the honorary 'capital' of the greater city that London has become. There is still a certain opposition between the City and Westminster. The City Corporation, having jealously guarded its rights and privileges for close on a thousand years, has maintained its independence to the present, surviving all reforms of London government in the Victorian period, and since, more or less intact. This independence was a source of irritation to progressive reformers in the 19th century no less than today; there are those who would echo the description of an exasperated Liberal who described it one hundred years ago as 'a sort of obsolete appendix at the centre [of London]'.

Though other boroughs have their own mayors and councils, the Lord Mayor is the Lord Mayor of London, and the Lord Mayor's Show, practically the last survival of the City's medieval pageantry, is a show for all Londoners. But the Lord Mayor, elected by and from the aldermen, is merely the creature of the City Corporation, whose writ runs no farther than the 667 acres of the City itself (plus some other districts, owned by the City elsewhere).

## Old and new

Another paradox: the City is at once the oldest and the newest part of London. Oldest as the site of the medieval city (and of the Roman town before that); newest because such a large proportion of it has been rebuilt within the past thirty or forty years. From a distance the extent of modern rebuilding – approximately nine-tenths since 1945 – can easily be seen, though once you enter it and explore the streets more closely it is surprising how many survivals of earlier ages still exist.

Curiously, much the same might have been said of the City a century ago. Then too it had recently undergone major reconstruction, the extent of which, by the end of the 19th century, was scarcely less than that of our own time. The major casualties then were the houses of the City merchants, many of them dating from a previous era of reconstruction in the generations after the Fire. They gave way in the Victorian period to offices, warehouses and other commercial premises, part of the long-continuing trend in the City towards workplaces and against residences. In fact, most of the old merchants' houses had been abandoned long before they were demolished, and many unwholesome districts disappeared as well as some fine (if decayed) old houses.

The Victorian City was also in decline – and in a few parts had already

disappeared – by the time the Blitz flattened a large part of it in a matter of months. The enormous pressure for more office space later put paid to much of what the bombs left standing. And yet if, for instance, you emerge into the City (as so many do daily) from the Underground station at the Bank, you find yourself in an environment that would be familiar in almost every detail to the City men of Queen Victoria's time.

Inside the banks and offices the changes have been remarkable, and here the most dramatic changes are postwar, the fruit of the contemporary revolution in communications. As for the people, they too have changed, constantly and sometimes dramatically. Without lingering over such ephemeral subjects as eating habits or fashions in dress, it is interesting to consider the career of the bowler hat.

## Badges of office

Taking up our position again at the entrance to the Bank Underground station in the morning rush hour in, say, 1958, and observing the hastening commuters, one notices that nearly every male head wears a bowler, as inseparable from the City gent as his rolled umbrella and *Financial Times*. Stand in the same spot a mere ten years later and, apart from the odd senior partner in some old-established family firm, the bowlers have disappeared as completely as the Victorian topper. The umbrella and *Financial Times* are still present, but we might notice other subtle changes; a larger number of women, for instance, and a greater proportion of them looking like executives rather than secretaries. Yet the sudden disappearance of the bowler from the heads of community allegedly hostile to change is one of life's little mysteries.

The aggrandisement of commercial property in the City affected other institutions. The diminishing population left many of the still numerous churches redundant. The vicar of St Clement's, Eastcheap, admitted with a touch of embarrassment in 1950 that he had no parishioners. A few City churches were destroyed: All Hallows, Bread Street, was demolished in 1876 and the parish merged with Bow. One of Wren's churches, ruined in the Blitz, was reconstructed on an American university campus. Others were put to nonparochial uses; variously active during the week, on Sundays their doors remain firmly locked against tourists and vandals.

Ancient educational institutions were also forced to move on. St Paul's School, founded by Dean Colet in 1509, vacated its premises in St Paul's Churchyard in 1884. It rose again, in glaring though imposing redbrick Gothic, in Hammersmith, but less than a century later the rising urban tide (in particular a new highway) forced it to move again, this time across the river to Barnes. Where will it be in another hundred years?

**King William Street,** *c.* 1900. King William Street was built as part of a 19th-century road improvement scheme, to provide easier access from the City to London Bridge, which was under construction at the same time (1829). At the far end, where King William Street meets Eastcheap, it is said that the Boar's Head tavern (prop. Mrs Quickly) stood, where Falstaff was accustomed to run up a vast bill for sack (fortified wine). Barely visible in the distance is the high column universally known as 'the Monument'. An informal street poll some years ago revealed that more than half those questioned did not know what it is a monument *to*. It commemorates, of course, the Great Fire, and was commissioned to stand 'on or as neere unto [as possible]' the spot where the Fire started.

## Holborn

Holborn was one of the first districts to be built up beyond the medieval city walls. Its name, like many London names, alludes to a waterway now vanished from sight, in this case the Fleet River.

The Fleet (its name comes from an old Anglo-Saxon word meaning a creek) must be the best-known invisible river (you can still follow much of its course underground) in the world. It was formed by the junction of two streams, one from Hampstead ponds, the other from Highgate, north of Regent's Park. It flowed south to Gray's Inn Road, took a turn towards Clerkenwell, then veered south again under Farringdon Road and Holborn (Holebourne – 'the stream in the hole') Bridge, where the land rose steeply on either side, finally reaching the Thames near Blackfriars Bridge. It gave its name to Fleet Street and the Fleet prison, and was once lined with sizeable wharves, but by the 18th century it had acquired an unsavoury reputation as Fleet Ditch, carrying not much trade but, according to Pope, a great quantity of dead dogs. In 1765, not long after a man had fallen in and been suffocated by the mud, it was filled in.

The valley of the Fleet in Holborn is now bridged by the famous Viaduct, an iron bridge over one hundred feet long which was the central element in a Victorian traffic-improvement scheme. It was opened by Queen Victoria in 1869, and the whole scheme, which included a great deal of demolition and reconstruction, cost over £2 million (not counting the cost of the new, though tiny, railway station built a few years later).

A large part of Holborn in early Victorian times was in no better condition, morally speaking, than the Fleet Ditch. About thirty years earlier Charles Dickens, then living in Doughty Street (the house is now a Dickens museum), had described the area in *Oliver Twist*. This was Fagin's stamping ground: the streets were 'very narrow and muddy, and the air . . . impregnated with filthy odours. There were a good many small shops; but the only stock in trade appeared to be heaps of childen . . . crawling in and out at the doors, or screaming from the inside. The sole places that seemed to prosper, amid the general blight of the place, were the public houses . . . Covered ways and yards, which here and there diverged from the main street, disclosed little knots of houses, where drunken men and women were positively wallowing in the filth; and from several of the doorways great ill-looking fellows were cautiously emerging, bound, to all appearances, on no very well-disposed or harmless errands.'

One advantage of the road improvement enforced by Victorian traffic congestion was that it also often involved a slum clearance, though the slum dwellers may not always have been happy about it. The pressing need

for easier north-south communication resulted in the construction, at the beginning of the present century, of Kingsway and its terminating crescent – a happy device – of Aldwych, which cut through a maze of mean streets and was soon adorned with monumental buildings (including Australia House, India House and Bush House, headquarters of the BBC overseas services). In Holborn itself some of the great Victorian edifices, like Gamages, disappeared fairly recently, though the great red castle of the Prudential Assurance Company looks safe for preservation, and some traces of the formerly more intimate aspect of Holborn remain in Leather Lane, site of a street market.

Like many other parts of London, Holborn has changed its character entirely in the past one hundred years. Its symbolic identity as the smallest metropolitan borough (including Bloomsbury) was finally abolished in the reorganization of local government in 1965, when it became part of the larger Greater London borough of Camden.

## Temple and Inns of Court

The chambers, apartments, offices, libraries and great halls of the legal profession lie on the border between the City and Westminster, a position, wrote G. M. Trevelyan, 'that helped the English lawyer to discover his true political function as mediator between Crown and people.'

The Temple owes its name to the Knights Templar, who existed in England from the early 12th century and built their round-naved church on its present site later in the same century (it was practically destroyed in the Blitz but has been lovingly restored). The order was suppressed in 1312 and its property passed to the Knights Hospitallers, who soon afterwards let part of the Inner Temple and the Middle Temple to two separate groups of lawyers. Their successors have remained there to this day, having successfully resisted the occasional attempts of the City to bring the Temple within its control (one visiting Lord Mayor was slightly roughed up).

The Temple was badly damaged in the Great Fire and in several

**The Turk's Head tavern,** near the Barbican, *c.* 1870. Early photographers were compelled to select static scenes because of the comparatively long exposure time required: hence the ghostly beer wagon here. Places tend to look underpopulated, especially by comparison with Victorian paintings, because people do not stay still. It was easier for photographers to focus on some unchanging subject, rather than, say a throng at a market. This vanished street north of the Barbican illustrates, among other things, the primitive character of butcher's shops in those days.

**The Strand** *1928*

subsequent fires, but the worst destruction was wrought by the Blitz. Someone picking his way through the ruins in 1942 remarked that the sundials were easier to read since so many buildings had come down. Someone else, having counted sixty species of wildflowers growing amid the rubble, observed that it was 'as good as Kew'.

Restoration was remarkably quick. The Middle Temple Hall, practically gutted in 1940 (though the hammerbeam roof survived), was back in use in 1949. Today there is little evidence of wartime disaster, and those who penetrate these well-concealed premises find themselves in a more tranquil world of gardens and courtyards.

The Victorian-Gothic Law Courts divide the Temple from the other two Inns of Court, Tudor Lincoln's Inn, where the young Dickens acquired his dislike of the legal profession, and, north of Holborn, Gray's Inn, where Francis Bacon kept chambers for fifty years. It too has been much restored after bomb damage, the hall, library and chapel having been completely rebuilt.

In general, the Inns of Court and the Temple, more than almost any other part of central London, convey an impression that one has strayed into the 18th century. Wigged lawyers seem to confirm it.

## Islington

Islington was a small rural village until the late 18th century, consisting only of a few houses grouped around the church at Islington Green (not much green left now). Nearby was a large 16th-century house, the tower of which has, remarkably, survived: Canonbury House, once the residence of Sir Francis Bacon, Oliver Goldsmith and Washington Irving. Now it is used as a theatre; like Southwark, Islington and Finsbury used to attract show-business people because they were outside, but not too far outside, the disapproving City. Islington remained a place for Londoners to go to have a good time (you could also see female boxing) until road improvements led to a spate of building from the 1760s.

Since becoming a residential borough Islington has passed through several identifiable phases. In the 19th century it was modest, respectable and inhabited largely by the aspiring middle class, though before the end of the century such people were moving farther out: the ineffable Mr Pooter moved his family to Holloway. In the early 20th century, after the ending of the Victorian leases, Islington dropped down the social scale, while growing a lot more lively, thanks largely to the presence of Irish workers. In our own time, new working-class housing has been built, and parts of Islington can be a shade raucous on Saturday night, but the old terraces have been gentrified, lovingly and expensively restored and filled with bric-a-brac from the dealers in Camden Passage.

## Clerkenwell

Clerkenwell is traditionally the home of jewellers, watchmakers and similar craftsmen, and even now they have not all been squeezed out. If you want someone to restore, say, an 18th-century barometer, you will probably find him in Clerkenwell.

The name means Clerks' Well, the clerks being not, of course, the City clerks who lived here in some numbers in the early 19th century, but the parish clerks of medieval London who met annually to perform their miracle

**The Oxford Arms,** Warwick Lane, c. 1874. The Oxford Arms off Newgate Street, closed its doors in 1875. It had been let out as cheap lodgings for some years prior to its final demise, but it had been a notable establishment before the railways drastically reduced its business as a transport terminus. At the height of the coaching age, about 1830-40, the proprietor of the Oxford Arms was Edward Sherman, one of the greatest of the coaching magnates, whose headquarters were at the Bull and Mouth, just around the corner, more or less.

play around the well. The well was still producing water that was 'extremely clear, sweet and well-tasted' in the 18th century; it became polluted in the 19th century, was closed over and lost to view, but rediscovered during excavations in 1924.

The frequency of the name 'St John's', not to mention 'Jerusalem Place', echoes Clerkenwell's long association with the Knights of the Order of St John of Jerusalem, founded in the 12th century when Clerkenwell was divided from the city by the swamps of Moorfields, a name now made familiar through another example of Clerkenwell's association with what is now called 'the caring profession', the famous eye hospital founded in 1805.

The Knights' priory was a large establishment occupying about ten acres south of Clerkenwell Green, where royalty and others were often entertained – at great expense, the prior was wont to complain. Wat Tyler burned a lot of it down and the Order was finally dissolved by Queen Elizabeth I. The remaining Knights repaired to Malta, their headquarters after the Order was thrown out of Jerusalem.

Unlike their wholly martial neighbours in the Temple, the Knights were originally a nursing profession rather than a military order, and the St John Ambulance Brigade was an offshoot of the revivified Order, founded in 1877. The distinctive white cross of the St John Ambulance men is the same as that worn by the medieval Knights.

The other great medieval institution of this district was Charterhouse, a Carthusian monastery and, from the early 17th century, site of the famous school. It moved to rural Godalming in 1872. Among its many distinguished former pupils was John Wesley, whose house and chapel still stand on City Road opposite the old burial ground of Bunhill ('Bone Hill') Fields.

Besides priests, scholars, literary men and the sick, Clerkenwell also looked after lunatics, the institution housed latterly in a fine 18th-century building designed by George Dance the Younger, also responsible for Finsbury Square. The building, next to St Luke's Church, was demolished in 1963; nothing remains of Dance's Finsbury Square either.

The most famous medical institution in this area, however, is St Bartholomew's Hospital in Smithfield, whose history is as old as the abbey founded in 1123, making it the oldest charitable institution in London still occupying its original site (the present buildings date from the reign of Queen Anne). The Church of St Bartholomew the Great is almost equally famous, the most notable London church to have survived since the high Middle Ages. It only narrowly escaped the bombs of the Second World War which, incidentally, brought to light a hitherto unsuspected Elizabethan half-timbered house in the gatehouse.

***Temple Bar*** *c. 1870*

**Temple Bar,** Fleet Street – Strand, *c.* 1870. 'Bar' as in Temple Bar means a barrier or post, such as were once placed across the gates to the City; the site of Holborn Bars is now indicated by granite posts near Staple Inn, and the site of Temple Bar, where the Strand becomes Fleet Street, is marked by an unprepossessing Victorian memorial including a bronze griffin. Temple Bar was especially significant because it lay on the road between the City and Westminster; royal visitors stopped here, to be admitted, after a brief ceremony, with the Lord Mayor's permission.

On these ceremonial occasions Temple Bar would be cleaned up and decorated. This was done in 1806, when new oak gates were installed, for Nelson's funeral; in 1863 for Princess Alexandra, wife of the future Edward VII; and for the last time in 1872, when Queen Victoria and her son went to St Paul's to give thanks for Prince Edward's recovery from typhoid.

There was a 'bar' here in the 13th century and probably much earlier, but the gate shown in this photograph of about 1870 was designed by Wren, with statues of Stuart monarchs by John Bushnell, and

***Temple Bar*** *today*

*The Staple Inn, Holborn 1875*

*Holborn today*

**Staple Inn, Holborn** is the most notable remnant of London houses dating from before the Great Fire. In the 1870s (left) it was plastered over; this was removed to reveal the Elizabethan half-timbering in 1886. It has often been restored , most recently in the 1950s after near-destruction by a flying bomb. Nevertheless, the façade at least is authentic. Pass through the old gateway to find an oasis of calm in the courtyard inside.

Today it looks more cared-for than it did in 1875 (it's a pity the Victorian street lamp has been scrapped) and its appearance is much the same as it was in 1586.

In the 15th century it was an Inn of Chancery, and it was purchased by benchers of Gray's Inn in 1529 – they retained control of it until the 19th century. In the 14th century it seems to have been for a short time a hostel for wool merchants – the 'merchants of the Staple' – which probably explains its name.

Samuel Johnson had lodgings for a time in Staple Inn, which never had much of a reputation among the greater Inns of Court. In the 1880s it was sold, the Tudor part passing into the possession of the Prudential Assurance Company, and they had it restored by the well-known architect, Alfred Waterhouse, who had recently designed the Pru's headquarters down the street.

erected in 1672. The earlier building had escaped the Great Fire, as it happened, but reconstruction was overdue anyway: Inigo Jones had designed a new gate in the 1630s but the Civil War intervened to prevent construction.

By the mid 19th century, however, the stranglehold that Temple Bar placed on traffic was already provoking demands for its removal. Less than one hundred years before, the heads (or other parts) of executed Jacobites had been displayed here, and such grisly associations diminished popular admiration for the structure. But these things take time, and it was not demolished until 1878. It lay about in bits in a builder's yard for a time, spent some years in Plumstead Marshes, and was finally re-erected on its present site in the rural seclusion of Theobald's Park, near Waltham Cross, once the property of King James I but at that time (1888) belonging to a brewing magnate.

**St Paul's from Ludgate Circus,** 1905. A good deal of repair and restoration has been necessary in this century, not all of it due to the effects of the Blitz, when devoted fire watchers saved St Paul's from major damage. Parts have had to be closed for long periods, and scaffolding temporarily obscured its grandeur until it emerged more magnificent than ever after cleaning.

We can feel little regret for the loss of the Victorian waterfront, a nasty muddle of decaying wharves and warehouses. What no photograph can do is to convey the frightful stench of the river, which was so strong that, a short way upstream, heavy curtains were drawn over the windows of the old House of Commons to defend the nostrils of the members.

The vast reconstruction evident in today's view was largely enforced by the Blitz, and on the whole there is again not much to lament, although the view up Ludgate Hill, photographed nearly fifty years later, casts doubt on the assertion by the developers responsible for the current environment of St Paul's that their trim though undistinguished buildings would obscure no more of the cathedral than had been visible originally. Ludgate Hill is just about recognisable here. The original Lud Gate has been lost to view since at least the mid 18th century and so, by the end of the 19th, had the Bell Savage (a corruption of Belle Sauvage, though the inn sign showed a savage and a bell), one of the most famous of London's coaching inns where, at its peak, some 400 horses were stabled. King Lud, commemorated in the Victorian tavern, was a mythical Celtic king who was said to have been responsible for an early version of London and was buried by Lud Gate. Hence, Lud's Town = London.

*St Paul's 1905*

*The same view today*

**St Paul's** today

**St Paul's Cathedral,** *c.* 1859 (overleaf). When this photograph was taken, London's great cathedral was approximately half its present age. Standing 365 feet high, on almost the highest point in the City, it still dominated the area, as Wren intended – and as its predecessor, the vast Gothic cathedral destroyed in the Great Fire, had also done. Built in the allegedly alien Baroque style traditionally regarded by the English as representing typical Catholic excess, it is nevertheless quintessentially English; its spacious, airy interior allows the Protestant congregation to see what is going on; no Popish mysteries here.

Wren had a struggle to push through his plans for St Paul's. The long nave was forced on him by the ecclesiastical authorities and there are other details not as intended, such as the gallery above the drum (Wren satirically remarked that ladies will have an edging to everything) and the missing clock in one of the west towers. Subsequent additions (all those Victorian monuments!) and deletions have not fundamentally affected the building.

While Westminster Abbey is a national church, St Paul's is the seat of the bishop of London and is more particularly a London church. It has, however, accepted its share of the bones of dead national heroes (and heroines), but tends to incline towards soldiers and artists, while the Abbey concentrates on statesmen and literary figures.

St Paul's was not generally open to the public until the first year of Queen Victoria's reign, and then with some widely expressed trepidation at the damage likely to be caused by the rabble. About the time this photograph was taken the original choir screen was removed to open up the interior still more – fears of vandalism having proved unfounded – to encourage larger congregations.

*St Paul's* 1859

*The same view today*

**St John's Gate,** Clerkenwell, *c.* 1875. Gatehouses with arches over the street were common enough in medieval London, but this is the only genuine survival, St John's Gate, once the entrance to the priory of the Knights of St John, erected, as an inscription informs us, in 1504, with stone from a Kent quarry. Rather satisfyingly for those of a conservative spirit, since the revival of the order in 1831 the gatehouse has again been occupied by the Order, which today is a charity concerned with voluntary hospital work, sending medical supplies to countries where they are needed, and the famous ambulance brigade.

The only other survival of the medieval order is the Norman crypt of the otherwise rebuilt church.

The gatehouse in this photograph of about 1875 is not quite as it was in earlier times, for it appears in one of W. Hollar's engravings of mid-17th-century London with an inner gate providing separate entrances for vehicles and pedestrians. The twin entries were still there after 1731, when it was occupied by Edward Cave's newly founded *Gentleman's Magazine*, which bore an engraving of the gatehouse on its title page. An early contributor to that fascinating publication was Samuel Johnson, not long up from Litchfield, who is said

*St John's Gate* c. 1875

*St John's Gate* today

to have worked in the chamber directly above the arch, hidden from visitors by a screen because his clothes were so disgracefully shabby. He brought another friend, David Garrick, here to give his first theatrical performance.

In the 19th century part of the gatehouse was occupied by The Old Jerusalem Tavern, and there was another famous inn farther up St John's Lane, The Baptist's Head. After the Order gained possession of the main building, a good deal of renovation was carried out. By the time of this photograph the battlements had been restored; the shields above the arch were replaced a few years later.

**Bishopsgate,** *c.* 1880. Today, walking up Bishopsgate, a main road to the north even in Roman London, one feels at times that one might be in sleekest Manhattan; pianomakers, coffee houses and pubs are less evident, banks much more so. Before the Great Fire, which in fact stopped just north of Leadenhall Street so that most of Bishopsgate escaped, it must have been still more attractive, if we may judge by the surviving façade of the Elizabethan house which is now in the Victoria and Albert Museum.

A piano was an essential ingredient in a Victorian (and later) middle-class home, in the same way as a TV set is now. Piano manufacturers in London before the First World War were numbered in hundreds. Messrs Moore and Moore were established in Bishopsgate around 1875, and their well-kept premises, with a fresh 'classical' façade disguising the somewhat shack-like quality of the building evident in the upper storey, only visible above street level, look reasonably prosperous.

Their claimed reputation 'for good and cheap pianos' would not be so stated now. What would be the modern equivalent? 'Instruments of high quality at moderate cost'? Our advertisers don't like talking about prices, and the word 'cheap' turns their pink cheeks white with horror. So much for Victorian hypocrisy.

*Bishopsgate c. 1880*

**Mansion House,** *c.* 1928 (overleaf) and the same view today. Rush hour in the City. The scene today is not so different in essence, though the buses now are less picturesque. Both the number and the routes of buses were regulated for the first time by the London Traffic Act of 1924, which was intended to reduce the number of buses on the streets yet not to discourage independent operators. The long-term effect was to encourage the 'General' – the word to be seen painted on the sides of buses and short for the London General Omnibus Company – which was the forerunner of London Passenger Transport.

In this photograph the majority of the buses visible have covered tops, yet this was a comparative novelty. The first covered-top bus had only appeared three years earlier.

The Mansion House itself, official residence of the Lord Mayor of London, was designed by George Dance, Clerk of the City Works. It was first occupied in 1752.

**Mansion House** 1928

**Mansion House** today

**London Bridge,** *c.* 1859, 1894 and today. Over a century ago the traffic on London Bridge in the rush hour was no less heavy than it is today, though different in character. A large industrial city entirely dependent for local transport on the horse was faced with problems no less intractable than the problems posed by modern motor traffic, and the noise was probably worse than the roar of contemporary traffic. People used to put down straw to deaden the sound of ironshod hooves and wheels on cobblestones.

The Victorian London Bridge was designed by John Rennie and opened in 1831, on the site of the medieval bridge famous in song and story which had supported

Above: *London Bridge* *1894*. **Below:** *London Bridge* *c. 1859*

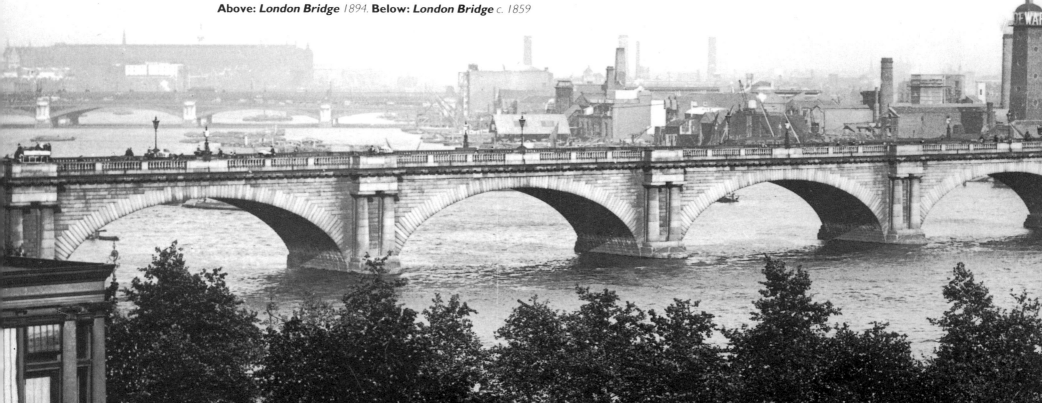

numerous buildings and shops (though fewer in its later days, a noticeable sagging towards the southern end having prompted precautionary demolition). Rennie's fine, solid piece of masonry would no doubt have lasted as long as its predecessor, given the chance, but it was too narrow – in fact it seems to have been too narrow for Victorian horse traffic, never mind buses and cars. It was replaced by the present three-span bridge in 1973. Rennie's bridge, carefully dismantled in 10,000 slabs of granite, was sold for over £1 million and re-erected over an artificial lake in the Arizona desert, a transaction which echoes those stories of New York con men selling the Brooklyn Bridge to innocent newcomers.

**London Bridge** *today*

**The Tower of London** *today and (right) c. 1890*

**The Tower of London,** *c.* 1890, and as it is today. The Tower of London has not changed significantly in the past century (though the cabs waiting on Tower Hill certainly have). Indeed, the White Tower itself, the original Norman building, has not changed very much in nine centuries. The rest of the medieval fortress was mostly built in the 13th century.

Tourist guides sometimes amuse themselves by letting imagination play upon the possible reasons for the name 'White Tower', but the true reason seems to be that in the Middle Ages it was painted white. (In the 1850s those guides' predecessors used to sell tickets to the unsuspecting 'to see the lions being washed'.)

The history of the Tower is long and mostly grim. Though it has served as a royal residence, an arsenal, a zoo, a defensive fortress and a museum, its best-known role is that of a political prison. Many traitors and alleged traitors spent their last days within its walls (one famous Jacobite escaped the day before his execution, disguised as a girl), most recently during the Second World War, when at least one spy was shot in the Tower, and Rudolf Hess spent a few days of what was to be a very long confinement.

The moat was drained in 1843 and sown with grass and shrubs, and since then the Tower has become largely a national monument and tourist attraction – a very popular one – with the picturesque Beefeaters in their Tudor uniforms, the tame ravens whose departure, it is said, will foretell the fall of the Tower, the ancient ceremony of the keys and of course the Crown Jewels, a vulgar display formerly on view in the Wakefield Tower but moved in 1967 to a specially constructed vault below the 19th-century Wellington Barracks. The Royal Fusiliers had moved out a few years earlier, though the Tower is still both a garrison and an arsenal.

A good many bombs and a couple of 'doodlebugs' fell in or around the Tower during the Second World War, but none of the ancient buildings was seriously damaged.

# WESTMINSTER
## AND THE WEST END
## CHAPTER TWO

London is still often regarded as a collection of villages which have gathered around two cities, the City of London and Westminster. The latter includes the loosely defined area of 'The West End', the part of London that the tourists know, the London of shops, hotels, theatres, art galleries, expensive dwellings and (increasingly since Victorian times) the headquarters of large commercial organizations. More important perhaps than even these attractive ingredients, Westminster is the home of government: since the 19th century the names 'Westminster' and 'Whitehall' have become synonyms for, respectively, parliament and government, or the civil service.

Westminster is younger than London (it only received its charter as a city at the beginning of this century!). It owes its origin to one of its most ancient buildings, the Abbey, built in the 13th-14th centuries but founded much earlier. As early as the 7th century there is supposed to have been a Saxon church on what was then called Thorney (i.e. 'brambly') Island, which was (like so many English 'isles') not strictly an island at all but probably – its precise boundaries have not been established – surrounded by ditches. The prosperity of the ancient abbey dates from the patronage of Edward the Confessor in the 11th century. Not only did Edward rebuild the Abbey on a lavish scale, but he also built his royal palace close by, thus originating the division between London (i.e. the City, Edward's former residence) and the Court.

## Crime and sanctuary

By the end of the Middle Ages Westminster was a densely inhabited, foul (the old name of Abingdon Street was Dirty Lane) and noisy town, also an unhealthy one due to its marshy site – a fine breeding ground for plague. It was beset by an extensive list of social problems, including a high crime rate. Although it was the royal capital, the medieval monarchy was a peripatetic institution, seldom remaining in Westminster, or anywhere else, for very long, so that those who earned an honest living in one way or another from the Court were compelled to maintain themselves in more irregular ways during the Court's absence. Another factor which contributed to Westminster's unsavoury reputation was the custom of sanctuary, by which fugitives were safe (sometimes!) from arrest while they remained within certain precincts. These included not only the Abbey itself but a much larger area round about. The name Broad Sanctuary, the street entering Parliament Square from the southwest, is a survival from these times, though Thieving Lane, no doubt an apt name, which once ran across the Westminster 'rookery' (a densely populated criminal slum) has disappeared.

Many street names record long-departed characteristics. Cockpit Steps commemorate our ancestors' more objectionable taste in entertainment; Petty France is said to have been colonised by French refugees though the French were there earlier in the shape of medieval wool merchants; Stuart kings maintained an aviary on Birdcage Walk; other names, like Caxton Street, Horseferry Road (the ferry was still in use in the 19th century) or Abbey Orchard Street are self-explanatory.

Although there was some extensive reconstruction in Georgian times, when Westminster Bridge was erected and the removal of the Court made it possible to widen Whitehall and extend Parliament Street, the Westminster rookery survived into Victorian times, when the modern plan of Westminster took shape.

**Marble Arch** was originally designed by Nash as the main entrance to Buckingham Palace based on the Arch of Constantine in Rome. It was removed in 1851 to its present position at the north-east corner of Hyde Park. It was never large enough to accommodate the traffic and the road was diverted around it in 1908.

## Victoria

The largest single feature of the Victorian replanning was Victoria Street, running slap through the old rookery, from the newly created Victoria Station (originally two stations, amalgamated with the aid of the Grosvenor, or Victoria, Bridge, the first railway bridge over the river) to Parliament Square. Victoria Street was lined on both sides with imposing buildings, including some of the earliest blocks of flats, of which Artillery Mansions (1895) still stand. The Victoria Palace Theatre, a music hall built in 1911, has also survived, but otherwise Victoria Street has been almost entirely rebuilt in recent years, though the vast modern office blocks that now confront and reflect each other above the traffic are no less imposing in their way than their Victorian predecessors.

Parliament Square itself was laid out on the site of a former slum; it was planned by Barry as an adjunct to his new Houses of Parliament. While Barry was devoting his talents to the legislature, other architects, such as Sir George Gilbert Scott, were doing their best for the civil servants north of Parliament Square. Parliament Street was widened, and is still said to be the widest street in London, though that seems to depend on how you define 'street'. Whitehall was already spacious – it had been wide enough in 1649 for the King to be executed on a temporary stage outside Inigo Jones's Banqueting House with a large crowd watching – though it was not linked with Parliament Street to form the present thoroughfare until 1899. The government offices marched all the way up to Charing Cross.

Vauxhall Bridge Road, which roughly marks the boundary between Westminster and Pimlico, was built in 1861 as a new main approach road to Vauxhall Bridge (1816), the first iron bridge in London, which replaced Rennie's unfinished stone bridge (iron was a cheaper medium).

## Pimlico

To the south Pimlico was a decidedly humble district until the Second World War, in spite of the nearby attractions of, successively, Ranelagh Gardens (pleasure gardens, demolished in 1805) and the Chelsea Flower Show in the grounds of Chelsea Hospital (still going strong). At about the

**Covent Garden,** Flower girls, *c.* 1895. The 'girls' were generally a great deal older than Eliza Doolittle in Shaw's *Pygmalion*. Their baskets, known as 'shallows', were usually hired at one penny a day, and the flowers they sold were posies or buttonholes which they made up themselves. Like other street traders, they adopted a conventional form of dress – white aprons, shawls and black hats.

beginning of the Victorian period Thomas Cubitt began building houses, much more modest than those he had raised in Belgravia, on what was largely wasteland, but they did not become fashionable. In the 1920s districts near the river were subject to flooding, and the odd citizen was drowned.

George Eliot and Joseph Conrad both lived, rather briefly, in Pimlico; a more characteristic resident of recent times was Anthony Powell's Maclintick, that bad-tempered but oddly sympathetic music critic. But the proximity of Pimlico to more desirable places (many MPs have had flats in Dolphin Square) plus a certain acquired period charm inevitably produced its recent upmarket progress.

A character in one of Trollope's novels considered that Eccleston Place was the southernmost point where one could contemplate living; she was not to be deceived into an address in Eccleston Square, the former being – just – in Belgravia, the latter indisputably and fatally in Pimlico.

In the early 18th century, someone leaving the tollgate at Hyde Park Corner would have found himself among fields and market gardens, the only substantial building being a mansion where St George's Hospital would be built. The gracious dwellings of Belgravia, centred on Belgrave Square, were planned and built by Cubitt, originally a Norfolk carpenter, from the 1820s onwards, after the area was drained and the River Westbourne converted to an underground sewer. Belgravia was intended to rival Mayfair as a fashionable residential district and, with the recent rebuilding of Buckingham Palace providing an attraction, it was successful from the first. It has largely retained its original character and appearance, although there are fewer dukes and earls in Belgrave Square, which in recent years has become the preserve of the diplomatic corps.

## The West End

The name 'West End' came into use in the 19th century to describe the fashionable district of London which is roughly defined by a line drawn today through Marble Arch, the Post Office (or Telecom) Tower, Charing Cross and Hyde Park Corner, with Piccadilly at its heart.

Piccadilly and Oxford Street were originally the two main roads leading from London to the west, and there were virtually no buildings of note on either of them until the 17th century. Piccadilly Hall, the house from which the street and circus derive their name, was the residence of a Jacobean merchant who is said to have made his fortune from selling a type of ruff called a picadil. The great noblemen's houses for which Piccadilly was later famous were built after the Restoration and the whole street was built up by

the mid 18th century. Burlington House is the only large house to have survived to the present. It was bought by the government in 1854, becoming the home of a number of learned societies and, most notably, of the Royal Academy, and it was considerably altered for the worse, notably by the addition of a second storey, in 1872. The virtues of the graceful Palladian building it once was have become hard to discern.

Rebuilding has gone on continually in Piccadilly. In the early 19th century it was the most exclusive residential street in London, as it remained until the discomforts of living on so busy a thoroughfare drove the rich residents out to Belgravia or other parts. Gentlemen's clubs moved into some former private houses; others were converted to offices. During the present century most of the clubs have also moved out, if not packed up altogether, and Piccadilly has become a place of business – of shops, hotels, banks and, more recently, airline and tourist offices. Few of the present buildings are more than one hundred years old, and some of the more modern ones tend to instil regret for the loss of the noble mansions of old, even if they had been as thoughtlessly treated as Burlington House.

## Oxford Street

Oxford Street, formerly 'Tyburn Way' among other names, was named, curiously enough, not because it was the road to Oxford (though it was) but because the land adjoining it was owned by the Earl of Oxford (Edward, son of Robert, Harley). Its character has changed completely since the 19th century. In about 1800 it was largely residential, most of the houses being comparatively recent, and it soon acquired a reputation as a place of entertainment. It was the site of the Princess's Theatre, where Ellen Terry made her first appearance and many of the great events of Victorian theatre took place, and of a skating rink, a building which, now housing the Salvation Army, still survives. The Princess's Theatre closed in 1902 but was not finally demolished until 1931, in favour of Woolworth's (itself since swept away).

The development of Oxford Street into the West End's largest shopping street, lined with great department stores, began before the end of the 19th

**Oxford Street,** *c.* 1900. This street, once known as Tyburn Way, has undergone a transformation more radical than all but a few of London's chief thoroughfares. Around 1800 it was largely residential, but now it is hard to find any remnant of a building predating the onset of the era of the department store in the late 19th century.

century, though the earliest, such as Marshall and Snelgrove, have not lasted till the present, when the solid, middle-class stores like Selfridges have increasingly found themselves harassed by cheaper competitors, often grouped in a single complex, such as Oxford Walk, which replaced the Woolworth's store. The street traders, mostly unlicensed and therefore illegal, have been there much longer.

The vast changes taking place on the main roads to the north and south during the 19th and 20th centuries have been much less notable in Mayfair, largely built up before the end of the 18th century and still retaining some Georgian elegance, as well as an aristocratic reputation, while the substantial areas reserved for carriages and horses (mews) have also moved up in the world, now providing bijou residences for fashionable actors, designers, and so on. Commerce has made considerable inroads since the 19th century, notably in the New Bond Street area.

## Covent Garden

Covent Garden was a rich residential area when first developed in the 17th century, but only for a few generations: more attractive housing to the west and the growth of the market lowered the tone, and in the 18th century Covent Garden was a rough district, with plentiful fights, minor riots even, and a large number of Turkish baths, the 18th-century equivalent of massage parlours. The market continued to grow as rival markets closed, but in an unorganised way, and the first specially designed structure was not built until the 1830s. More – the Floral Hall, the Flower Market, etc. – followed, together with closer supervision, though there were still many complaints.

Suggestions of an alternative site for the market had been made frequently since the 18th century, but it was not until 1974 that it finally moved out, to derelict former railway property at Nine Elms in Battersea. Under G.L.C. supervision, old Covent Garden was restored and turned into a high-class tourist trap, full of small, specialised, expensive shops and restaurants, with the London Transport Museum, most recently located in Syon Park, housed in the refurbished Flower Market.

East of Tottenham Court Road, Bloomsbury was also Bedford property, and an aristocratic residential area in the 17th century, built up in its familiar squares and terraces in the early 19th and then attracting writers and artists. Until 1893 the self-contained character of Bloomsbury's squares was emphasised by gates which shut them off from the rest of the world.

By that time Bloomsbury was becoming less fashionable, though still respectable, and the trend continued in the 20th century in spite of the presence of members of the Bloomsbury Group, in a manner familiar from other districts: population declining, houses being demolished (though some of Georgian Bloomsbury has survived) and other institutions moving in. The most famous of these is the British Museum, founded in 1755 in what had been Montagu House. Robert Smirke's classical building replaced it in the 1830s; the famous Reading Room was more or less an afterthought, created by raising a dome over the courtyard. The University of London, starting off on a very small scale in Somerset house in 1826, engorged a good deal of Bloomsbury when the modern buildings, including the Senate House, were built between the wars.

**Covent Garden,** *c.* 1890 and the same scene today (below). The market then is much as Dickens described it, 'an hour after daybreak', when the market and nearby streets 'are thronged with carts of all sorts, sizes and descriptions, from the heavy lumbering wagon, with its four stout horses, to the jingling costermonger's cart, with its consumptive donkey. The pavement is already strewed with decayed cabbage-leaves, broken hay-bands, and all the indescribable litter of a vegetable market; men are shouting, carts backing, horses neighing, boys fighting, basket-women talking, piemen expatiating on the excellence of their pastry, and donkeys braying.'

## Mayfair

The rise of Mayfair was achieved largely at the expense of areas farther east, Soho and Covent Garden in particular, which had formerly been the most fashionable residential districts. Soho, once hunting land (the origin of the name is supposed to be an old hunting cry), later supported a handful of great houses, on whose estates speculative building began in the 17th century. Its modern cosmopolitan reputation was established fairly early, when French Huguenots settled in the area in such numbers that French was heard in the streets more often than English. Many other foreigners arrived later. Artists, another traditional Soho group, were present in some numbers before 1800, and by about 1850 Soho was so crowded (and accordingly unhealthy) that the wealthier residents had moved out.

**Rotten Row,** *c.* 1915. Hyde Park, a royal deer park in the 16th century, was first opened to the public by King Charles I about 1635, and it is from that time that its popularity as a place for driving and riding by the fashionable world dates. The sandy, tree-lined Rotten Row (a corruption of *route du roi*), or 'the Row', was originally part of a road leading from Kensington Palace to St James's. Before the end of the 17th century it was lit at night with lamps hung from trees, surely the earliest example of street lighting in England though this did not stop highwaymen.

In the 19th century the paths beside Rotten Row were a fashionable rendezvous after church on Sundays. The tradition had not died out by the First World War, when this photograph was taken, although royalty were unlikely to be present and more people arrived in cars than broughams. Today, Rotten Row provides nearly a mile of brisk trotting.

Soon afterwards Soho began to gain its reputation as a place of entertainment, including entertainment of a disreputable sort. Restaurants came later; although they were mentioned as a characteristic of the district before the end of the 19th century, Soho did not become the place to seek one's dinner after the theatre until the 1920s. In spite of this intrusion of the English middle class Soho remained a scruffy, foreign, lively sort of place, although after the Second World War its resident population, already in decline, fell to two or three thousand.

## Kensington

Most of Kensington was occupied by market gardens and orchards up to the 19th century, although to the north, towards Notting Hill, a number of large houses, country estates in effect, were built during the 17th century. One of the first and largest was Holland House (about 1610), a great centre of society in the 19th century, so much so that parts of the estate had to be sold off to pay for the lavish entertainment of the Holland family; hence Holland Park. The house was reduced to a ruin by bombs in the Blitz and afterwards purchased by the L.C.C., who restored as much of it as seemed feasible.

In 1689 King William III, disliking Whitehall, had Nottingham House converted into a royal palace; most of the great architects of the period, from Wren to Colen Campbell, worked on it at different times, but in the late 18th century it fell into neglect because George III preferred Buckingham Palace. Repairs were effected for the Duke of Kent (father of Queen Victoria, who was born there), and ever since it has served as a royal residence – for instance for Princess Margaret.

The presence of the Court spurred the development of Kensington into a rural suburb inhabited by 'persons of quality', but it did not begin to grow really fast until the 19th century – from about, 8,000 in 1801 to about 176,000 in 1901. Many of the larger houses were retained, serving as schools or lunatic asylums, but the former market gardens were covered by a dense network of streets. The confidently ornate estate of Kensington Court, built in the 1880s, was supplied with electricity from a private generating station, whose building still stands.

Still more remarkable were 19th-century developments in South Kensington, in the great complex of museums which stand together as a mighty monument to the Victorian belief in the importance of knowledge and education in social progress. Presiding over them was placed the memorial to Prince Albert: he epitomised the whole idea and provided the initiative for the creation of what became the Victoria and Albert Museum. With a few – some, such as the recent wing of the Natural History Museum, rather startling – additions, these great institutions have hardly changed in the past century, though changing fashions in exhibitions have dramatically altered what goes on inside, notably in the Science Museum, which sometimes looks like a kind of didactic fun fair and attracts hoards of schoolchildren.

Rather difficult developments took place to the north of the Royal Borough (the title was granted in 1901), in the district known as Notting Hill. The old gravel pits and the farms of Portabello and Notting disappeared under houses between the 1830s and 1870s. From the first this was a district of startling contrasts, with fine houses and dreadful slums in close proximity. This is broadly the situation today, though the slums are not quite so bad and the fine houses are fewer. A large number of West Indian immigrants settled hereabouts in the 1950s, and one result of this new element is the now annual Notting Hill street carnival.

**The Albert Memorial.** The design of the Albert Memorial was chosen by Queen Victoria from a number of designs submitted by the most notable architects of the day. The winner was George Gilbert Scott and the whole edifice cost £120,000, which seems a bargain nowadays, even if the thing is an outstanding piece of Victorian kitsch.

**Regent Street,** *c.* 1895, and the same view today. Regent Street was probably the single grandest, planned street in London, a stately way leading from Carlton House, home of the Prince Regent, to Regent's Park. Unfortunately, Nash's whole splendid plan was never perfectly achieved, since before it was finished some parts had already been knocked down! Lower Regent Street, the first section on which Nash's fine yet unpretentious stucco-fronted houses arose, was quick to decline into the rather nondescript character it has now, and the splendid Carlton House itself, scene of the Prince Regent's most lavish entertainments, was the first casualty, as the Prince on becoming king had no further use for it. On the site, however, Nash built Carlton House Terrace, which has survived.

In Nash's original scheme (considerably qualified in execution in order to satisfy various vested interests), Regent Street was mainly residential, with shops being concentrated in the Quadrant, immediately north of Piccadilly Circus. This section today, though rebuilt, retains a suggestion of elegance (not all the original buildings were designed by Nash himself, but he kept overall control of the general scheme).

By the end of the 19th century, Regent Street had already begun to change. Although a few buildings had gone completely, the changes were mostly social and economic rather than architectural. The street was moving a shade down-market and was no longer the centre of fashionable society.

Reconstruction had also become necessary, since the old buildings were in poor shape. Structural soundness is not usually listed among Nash's many fine qualities,

***Regent Street***

***Regent Street*** c. 1895

*Carlton House Terrace*

and the shops. spreading up the street, had undertaken some ill-advised alterations to increase space. In 1907 Norman Shaw's Piccadilly Hotel arose in the Quadrant, and the huge Regent Palace Hotel (1,000 rooms) was in business by mid-1915; it was soon packed with officers on leave from the trenches. Shaw's plans for a unified scheme extending along much of Regent Street were rejected. Nevertheless, Regent Street was virtually rebuilt entirely by the end of the 1920s, after building restrictions had been lifted, and with generally higher roof lines – an aspect of Shaw's plans which had aroused particularly fierce objections.

The new Regent Street did not meet with universal approval, but it remained, as it is today, a splendid shopping street, and there are still a few businesses there, such as the Café Royal or Hedges and Butler, which were established long before the reconstruction.

*Oxford Circus* c. 1915

**Oxford Circus**

**Oxford Circus,** c. 1915. Oxford Circus can claim to be, more or less, a true circus, as Piccadilly once was but has long since ceased to be, the façades of the buildings on the corners of the Regent Street/Oxford Street crossroads being curved. Oxford Circus was built a century after Nash's time, during the reconstruction of Regent Street. When this photograph was taken, the other side of the Circus was still unfinished. The architect was Sir Henry Tanner, one of the busiest Edwardian architects, whose other buildings in Regent Street included the Regent Palace Hotel, Dickens and Jones (rebuilt 1921, on the corner of Great Marlborough Street), and the rebuilt Café Royal.

By this time, the last of the horse-drawn omnibuses had long vanished and the internal combustion engine, or, as someone remarked speaking of city traffic, the internal congestion engine, had taken over completely. In spite of street widening the traffic situation became so bad in this area after the Second World War, aggravated in Oxford Street itself by the masses of shoppers overlapping the kerbs, that in the 1970s the West End's busiest shopping street, though also a major east-west artery, was made into a limited access road for vehicles. However, buses and taxis were admitted, and at busy junctions north-south traffic continued to pass through, so that the end result has proved to be something less than the calm, tree-lined, pedestrian precinct that some planners had dreamed of.

**Bond Street,** *c.* 1895. The division between Old and New Bond Street, which occurs at just about this spot, at the junction with Grafton Street, does not signify any very great difference in age since both parts were built up in the early 18th century, though Old Bond Street was finished earlier.

Bond Street was a fashionable promenade with expensive shops from the first, although the actual buildings were (and are) nothing special and the street was (and is) inconveniently narrow. Yet all the famous names are still here – Agnew's, Wildenstein's, Cartier's, Sotheby's, Mappin and Webb and many more.

***Bond Street*** *today*

***Bond Street*** *c. 1895*

**Piccadilly and Green Park,** c. 1890. The widening of Piccadilly at the Hyde Park end took place soon after 1900, and one incidental result was a shrinkage of the acreage of Green Park, on the south side of the street, the railings of which had to retreat in order to accommodate the new roadway. A good deal of excitement was caused by the rumour that London County Council intended to cut down some of the large trees, though in fact this was unnecessary (nevertheless, it is apparent from this photograph that *some* trees must have been removed). Trees on the pavement outside the park railings were planted after completion of the reconstruction.

Opposition to the diminution of the park was partly responsible for the road being widened less than was desired. At about the same time the Broad Walk which now cuts across Green Park was created as an adjunct to the Victoria Memorial. The 18th-century iron gates at the Piccadilly end of the Broad Walk, erected in 1921, came from Devonshire House (demolished in 1924), though they had had more than one home before that.

Green Park is a peaceful enough place now, frequented by footsore tourists and sandwich-eating, lunchtime office workers; but in the 18th century the park was the favoured site for duelling among West End swells, and was also a resort of highwaymen.

*Piccadilly today*

*Piccadilly* c. 1890

***Piccadilly Circus*** *today*

the aluminium statue above a drinking fountain (the cups were soon pinched as souvenirs) supposed to represent the Angel of Christian Charity, which was created as a memorial to the philanthropic Earl of Shaftesbury (after whom also Shaftesbury Avenue was named) by Alfred Gilbert in 1890-93. It rapidly became the best known and most affectionately regarded work of art in London, though the sculptor, having quarrelled with the Board of Works, refused to attend the

**Piccadilly Circus,** 1910 and *c.* 1895 (overleaf). If 'circus' is supposed to imply circular, then it is no longer an appropriate word today at Piccadilly Circus, except below the surface, where the well-planned, recently-renovated Underground station adopts that form. Otherwise, Piccadilly Circus has long been a dreadful muddle, the subject of innumerable schemes for improvement (or for making the planners a lot of money) all of which it has defied more or less successfully.

It came into existence as a result of Nash's Regent Street scheme in the early 19th century and was then a simple crossroads; but the buildings of the four corners each had a concave facade, hence the 'circus'. It looks very elegant in coaching prints of the 1830s and 1840s, though perhaps a little congested even then. The symmetry was for ever destroyed by the formation of

Shaftesbury Avenue from a number of smaller, linked streets in the 1880s. The London Pavilion was built at that time, replacing an older building, and its Victorian neoclassical facade, on the north-east side of the Circus, remains to this day. The terms of the leases on the new buildings, in the spirit of Victorian *laisser faire*, were less strict than the old leases, with the result that the London Pavilion and its neighbours discovered that no one could prevent them from covering the property with illuminated signs. Bovril and Schweppes were flashing merrily above the growing snarl of the traffic as early as 1910, shortly before the Regency version of Swan and Edgar disappeared. Regency elegance had gone altogether by 1914; in exchange, the Circus gained a certain brash vigour and excitement.

It did owe something to Eros, the popular name for

opening ceremony. 'Flower girls' used to sit around it (their place taken since the 1950s by representatives of international blue-jeaned youth), and Mrs Emma Baker held station there for 57 years, by which time flower *girl* was hardly the right description.

Eros, freshly installed in this photograph of about 1895, has taken leave of absence on several occasions: between 1923 and 1929, when further alterations to the Circus were taking place, he was in the

Embankment Gardens; during the Second World War he was evacuated to Egham; recently, the figure had to be removed from sight for extensive restoration.

Whereas the London Pavilion has recently been cleaned up, the building opposite housing the Criterion Theatre (the first theatre built underground, 1874) typifies the scruffiness with which, despite all the best intentions, Piccadilly Circus has been indelibly identified since the early years of this century.

**Piccadilly Circus** *c. 1910*

*Piccadilly Circus* c. 1890

*Piccadilly Circus* 1973

**The Strand,** *c.* 1895 and 1908. The Strand links Westminster to the City, where it becomes Fleet Street. Originally a riverside path, it became a genuine 'street' in the 16th century when the houses of lords and bishops were built there. In the 17th century smaller houses replaced them and the first shops appeared. In the 18th century the Strand was famous for coffee houses; Twining, the tea merchant, was there in Queen Anne's reign, and his firm still is. In the 19th century the western end of the Strand was transformed; the old Charing Cross Hospital, by Decimus Burton, was built in the 1830s (it moved to

Fulham in 1973), Charing Cross Hotel in the 1860s, the Savoy and the Cecil Hotel in the 1880s.

The Strand also contained more theatres than any other London street. One or two are still there, but not, unfortunately, the Gaiety, which was demolished in 1957 to make room for what is now called Citibank House (formerly the headquarters of the English Electric Company). The original Gaiety, seating 2,000 not including the popular restaurant and stretching from Exeter Street to Catherine Street, opened in 1868, replacing the old Strand Music Hall, and it was the first theatre to have an electrically illuminated façade

(1878). It was famous for burlesque shows. In the 1890s the famous Gaiety Girls attracted numerous wealthy young men, bearing flowers, to the stage door, and it is said that a large proportion of the chorus girls ultimately married rich and aristocratic husbands.

In 1900 the Strand was widened as part of a major improvement scheme which involved the demolition of the buildings on the northern side of the eastern part of the Strand. The old Gaiety was among the casualties, closing in 1903, but the new Gaiety, partly designed by Norman Shaw, opened only a few months later, on the corner of the new Aldwych. When the old Gaiety was

*The Strand c. 1895*

demolished, a vast horde of rats was released. They invaded the restaurant, causing considerable consternation – and damage – but were eventually driven back into the sewers whence they had come.

These photographs show the Strand looking towards the church of St Mary-le-Strand (by James Gibb, 1717), in about 1895, before the widening of the Strand; in about 1908, after the improvements, and shortly before omnibuses finally drove their horse-drawn competitors from the streets; and in 1989, with only the church – which has taken shelter on an island – recognisable in all three photographs.

*The Strand* c. 1908

*The Strand* today

**Buckingham Palace** c. 1900

**Buckingham Palace,** *c.* 1900. The history of the construction of Buckingham Palace, the Queen's residence in London, is something of a saga. It began life as a relatively modest dwelling, Buckingham House, built for the Duke of Buckingham in 1703 on a piece of land granted to him by Queen Anne. The site came back into royal possession when the house was bought by King George III in 1762.

When the Prince Regent became King George IV in 1820 he decided that Carlton House was not half grand enough for him and suggested a new palace to replace Buckingham House (then known as Queen's House, Pimlico), to which he was sentimentally attached. He estimated the job could be done for half a million

*Buckingham Palace today*

pounds, about three times as much as the government was willing to spend. Sir John Soane proposed a more modest building in Green Park, but George IV insisted on the original site and on John Nash as the architect.

Costs spiralled; the prime minister (Wellington) at one point exclaimed that he was damned if he would pay for some extra expenses required by Nash. The building was not ready for George IV, who died in 1830, nor for his brother William IV (died 1837) and not, really, for Queen Victoria, although she moved in – and liked it (later she would pine for a Highland croft).

Meanwhile Nash had been dismissed (1830), having rather asked for it by his exceedingly unhelpful replies to a parliamentary committee investigating the reasons for the mounting bills. He was replaced by Edward Blore, who was responsible for the public face of the palace completed in 1846, as seen in this photograph –

not at all according to Nash's design, which was for an open courtyard. This made it necessary to shift Marble Arch from its position in front of the palace to its present site at the north-east corner of Hyde Park.

It is a pity that Nash's plans were not fulfilled, all the same, as anyone will agree who has seen the much more attractive rear façade of the Palace (Nash's work), which is unfortunately invisible to the public (as is the interior) except those who are invited to royal garden parties.

Blore's rather pathetic frontage disappeared in 1913, when the whole eastern façade, later to become familiar throughout the world through television broadcasts of royal occasions, was rebuilt in warm Portland stone by Sir Aston Webb, the architect also of Admiralty Arch, at the other end of the Mall, and of the Victoria and Albert Museum in South Kensington.

**High Street, Kensington,** *c.* 1899. The High Street, which could still be described as a 'picturesque' village street at the time of the First World War, has changed completely in character and appearance. Many parts have been rebuilt at least twice although, especially just off the High Street, many of the earlier buildings remain, notably some very distinctive Victorian flats. Generally speaking, however, the High Street has become a cosmopolitan shopping street, second only to Oxford Street and Regent Street.

Essentially this transformation took place between the wars, but most of Kensington's famous stores can be traced back a long way further. John Barker had a drapery shop here in the 1870s, and Barker's department store was built before the First World War. Pontings was also present in the 1870s; it expanded to incorporate two former aristocratic mansions, which were subsequently demolished to make room for the late Victorian department store, was later bought by Barker's, and was demolished in turn in the 1970s. Derry and Toms arose next to Barker's in 1933, but that too was an old business, Messrs Toms and Derry having amalgamated in 1862. The store became famous for its roof garden, where sizeable trees now grow. When Derry and Toms closed in 1973 it was taken over by Biba, who turned it into a 'dream emporium', but Biba's neo-Art-Deco dream lasted only two years before the store passed into more mundane hands.

In this photograph, taken from the junction with Kensington Church Street about 1899, and looking east, not much is familiar ninety years later. The Royal Palace Hotel was less than ten years old then. Seifert's Royal Garden Hotel replaced it in 1965.

*The old 'Civet Cat' pub sign*

*High Street Kensington c. 1899*

*High Street Kensington today*

***Marylebone Road*** *c. 1959*

***Marylebone Road*** *today*

**Marylebone Road,** *c.* 1959. Anyone compelled to drive along Marylebone Road regularly in the 1990s must feel envious of this uncluttered view, photographed thirty years ago. Known as New Road until 1857, it was built one hundred years earlier in accordance with an act of parliament requiring a 'new road' between Islington and Paddington. George Shillibeer's original 'Omnibus' ran on it, much harassed by coachmen, in 1829. In the 1890s it was described as a grimy thoroughfare, but it has been almost entirely rebuilt since then.

Mme Tussaud arrived in England to exhibit her waxworks (mainly heads of victims of the French Revolution) in 1802, but it was not until 1835 that her show was permanently established in Baker Street. In 1884 the museum, then consisting of some 400 figures, moved around the corner to its present site in Marylebone Road, but the building burned down in 1925, with the loss of many waxworks but fortunately not the casts. The present building was purpose-built for the collection. The contents have changed a good deal over the years: the Chamber of Horrors, even in the 1950s, was a lot more horrid (it must have given many children nightmares), while the recreation of historical events such as the Battle of Trafalgar with sound and light effects has added an extra dimension.

The Planetarium, just visible next door, opened in 1958, with a Zeiss projector capable of displaying 9,000 stars on the dome. Nowadays, displays with laser light are also shown.

# THE RIVER DOWNSTREAM

## CHAPTER THREE

The River Thames is in a sense London's *raison d'être*. The reason why a town arose on the site in the first place was because it was the first convenient spot upstream to cross the river. And the river nourished it, providing it with goods and services on a generous scale.

The Thames is not a particularly distinguished river, a lowland waterway of moderate size, not much more than 200 miles in length and only about 250 yards across at London Bridge. Its daily flow may be as little as 200 million gallons, and though after heavy rains it may be 100 times as much, the Amazon despatches more than that into the Atlantic in less than five minutes.

However, if the Thames made London possible, London has repaid the Thames by making it famous. It's a safe bet that no other river in the world, with the possible exception of the Nile, has had more words written about it.

The Thames flows through the rich countryside of the southern Midlands, traditionally bringing food and raw materials to the city, and the estuary forms a gateway to the continent, bringing European trade within easy reach of London.

So far as London is concerned, the Thames is essentially an estuary, Teddington Lock marking the limit of the tidal river nearly twenty miles above London Bridge (though the ebb tide is held up by Richmond Lock). Throughout the Tidal reach, the water becomes gradually less salty, less well oxygenated and cooler. Normally, freshwater, being lighter, flows above sea water, but in the tidal Thames there is an unusually good 'mix', probably due to the numerous sharp bends which have the effect of swinging the main current from bank to bank.

## Tributaries

In addition to the main stream flowing from the Cotswolds, the tidal Thames receives freshwater from many tributaries, which have also played their parts in the historical growth of London. Those within Greater London are the Crane (Twickenham), the Brent (Brentford), Beverley Brook (Putney), the Wandle (Wandsworth), the Ravensbourne (Deptford), the Lea (Bow) which is much the largest, the Roding (Barking), the Beam and the Ingrebourne (Rainham), the Darent (Dartford) and the Mardyke (Purfleet). This list excludes various man-made channels of one sort or another, and vanished rivers such as the Fleet and the Tyburn.

In recent times all these streams were mainly carriers of sewage, and thirty years ago virtually all, at least in their lower reaches, were seriously polluted. Since the 1960s they have been greatly improved. Even the Wandle, which is still in fact a sewer, now supports some wildlife, though it is rather far from regaining its former distinction as a trout stream.

Londoners have made many uses of the Thames and its tributaries besides the supply of freshwater and the transport of effluent. For example, in the 18th century the river was dotted with watermills, though the irregular flow raised problems in the tidal river, sometimes necessitating an artificial channel in which the flow could be more easily regulated. The Wandle, with its relatively steep fall, was particularly suitable for water-powered industry (for the same reason it was not much good for navigation). In the early 19th century this little river supported twelve calico printing works, nine flour mills, five snuff mills and a number of other enterprises such as tanning and papermaking – surely a record for its size.

## Transport

Until comparatively recent times the Thames was a vital highway. It is said that in the 18th century Reading, for example, depended on the river to transport more than 90 per cent of goods entering and leaving the town. The Thames must often have been packed with slow-moving barges, loaded to the gunwales with grain, malt or timber, making their way towards the capital. The quantity of this traffic forced the authorities to improve navigation in various ways, such as construction of pound locks (the first dated from the reign of Charles II, though this was rather tardy by European standards, such devices having been in use in France and Germany three hundred years earlier). Navigational improvements, assisting ships but not salmon, were probably responsible, along with pollution, for the extinction of migratory fish from the Thames.

On the lower river the shipping was generally larger; barges towed by horses (or men) were not a practical proposition there, and in the late 18th century there emerged the distinctive and beautiful Thames sailing barge, fore-and-aft rigged, round-bowed, with a special arrangement to lower and raise the mast quickly when shooting a bridge, and of such shallow draught that they were said to be able 'to sail over a heavy dew'. One nautical historian described them as 'the most highly specialized and efficient cargo-carriers ever evolved'. Unfortunately, like the stagecoach, they were becoming obsolete within a very short time of reaching perfection. Yet for some time they could be seen in dozens, bringing grain, vegetables and other produce, via the Medway, from the farms of Kent.

**Millwall Docks** *c.* 1919. Dockers unloading a cargo of coir, used for making netting and cordage.

## The watermen

The late 17th and 18th centuries saw the heyday of the Thames watermen, one of the most interesting of the historic trades of London. Because London Bridge was the only crossing in the capital until Westminster Bridge was built in 1750, people had to cross the river by boat, and the river was also the best route if you were going any distance east-west, or from the City to Westminster. Boats of many kinds could be hired, from single scullers up to what amounted to river omnibuses, with six or eight oars.

The watermen were a clannish bunch, who used to vie with each other, as they passed in midstream, in a contest of colourful cursing, and they were even willing to indulge in rhetorical exchanges with such as Samuel Johnson. The Company of Watermen and Lightermen became so concerned at passengers' complaints of bad language that a ban was imposed, with fines for offenders.

The best known of the watermen is John Taylor, self-styled 'the Water Poet', one of the most attractive figures in subliterary history. He engaged in a long verbal war against coaches, which the watermen of the late 17th century saw as a threat to their livelihood. If the Water Poet was upset by coaches, which in fact had little effect on the watermen's trade, what would

he have said to the bridges which began to span the river at frequent intervals from the late 18th century? Or to the railways, or, finally and most fatally, to the steamboats of the 19th? By the late 19th century the trade of the watermen, and, since the building of the docks, of the lightermen who carried goods between ship and quay, had shrunk to almost nothing. Nevertheless, the Company of Watermen and Lightermen still exists, and a few people still make their living as boatmen on the tidal Thames.

## Shipbuilding

Another trade that entered a decline in the 19th century was ship-building, but this was at least partly a corollary of the growth in London's trade, reflected in the construction of the series of enormous docks from Wapping to Woolwich between 1800 and 1920. The London dockers could be regarded as the successors of the old watermen and lightermen, with many similar characteristics, but their trade too is now almost defunct: the closing of the West India Dock in 1908 symbolised the end of an era.

Industry also increased on the lower Thames along with trade, especially in districts like Silvertown and the Isle of Dogs, which was all green pasture before the docks were built. The derelict docklands have recently emerged in a very different role, as a fashionable residential area, with their own railway and airport and a sprinkling of light industry and commerce.

**Wapping,** London Docks, c. 1907. Officials of the Revenue service are inspecting wine barrels. The officer who measured the contents of barrels was called a gauger. The shipment in the foreground consists of a 'parcel' of five hundred pipes of Tarragona wine, shipped by Gilbey Vintners. The gentlemen standing nearby have been identified as Gilbeys' representative and the vault keeper. Behind them is a further shipment, of Spanish brandy in hogsheads. The curious square turrets on the right are box cranes: the hydraulic machinery was contained in the boxes.

**Thamesmead,** c. 1865. The Crossness sewage works were constructed on Belvedere marshes in the early 1860s. They were designed by that industrious engineer, Sir Joseph Bazalgette, for the Metropolitan Board of Works and covered an area of 37 acres. Discharging an average of 70 million gallons a day, they were located far enough below the capital not to offend Londoners. However, from 1887 the sludge was offloaded into ships for dumping at sea; only the – relatively – inoffensive effluent was discharged direct into the river. Today, no nasty smells assail the nostrils of the people of nearby Thamesmead, the 'new town' still growing on the former marshes.

## Drinking water

Of all the purposes to which Londoners have put their river and its tributaries, the longest-lasting is that of the water supply. In the Middle Ages most of London's water was drawn directly from wells and rivers, although as early as the 13th century some water was conducted in wooden pipes from the Tyburn to the City. In 1581 an ingenious Dutchman, Pieter Morice, installed a water wheel in one of the arches of London Bridge, which pumped water to the City, and although the waterworks were destroyed in the Great Fire, they were afterwards rebuilt and survived until the bridge itself was rebuilt in the 1820s. (Latterly, the water was admitted to be foul, but after standing for 24 hours it was said to be as fine as any water available, which may be seen as a dire comment on the general standard.)

The New River was built early in the 17th century, a great improvement although quite costly – customers paid £1 6s a year. From about this time water, which had once been free, was largely supplied by such commercial companies, which failed to measure up to the fairly high standard set by the New River Company. Many of them drew water from the Thames below Chelsea, and at first it was completely untreated. They were more interested in profits than in providing a decent service, as is often the way with such enterprises. Their profits were considerable, their water was nasty. As

someone remarked, many Londoners were paying to drink their own waste.

The Metropolitan Water Act of 1852 ended the worst abuses of the water companies: it was henceforth forbidden to draw drinking water from the Thames below Teddington, and filtration was made compulsory. Legislation is one thing, law enforcement is another, however, and the penalties were small compared with profits. As a parliamentary committtee had reported, with suspect moderation, Thames water 'cannot . . . be pronounced entirely free from the suspicion of general insalubrity'. Not long after this (in 1858) the windows of the House of Commons were covered with curtains soaked in chloride of lime against the stench of the river.

## Waste disposal

Matters were not improved by the ancient but vigorously sustained custom of getting rid of all forms of rubbish – dead cats, butchers' refuse, rotten food, excrement – by dumping it in the nearest waterway. It was this habit which accounted for the noxious state of the Fleet River, a subject of complaint as early as the 13th century, and other tributaries. At one time latrines were positioned on the bridge at Holborn so that human excrement could drop straight into the stream.

Water supply was also extremely variable in quantity. In some poor districts it was only available – from a stand pipe – for less than half an hour a day, and not at all on Sundays. Efforts at reform constantly came to nothing, part of the trouble being, as the great reformer Edwin Chadwick complained, that a very large number of MPs were shareholders in the water companies. The solution, was finally put into effect in 1902 when the private companies, whose record, with a few exceptions, was truly appalling, were taken over by the Metropolitan Water Board. The Board embarked upon a big programme of reservoir building and in a few years all Londoners received a constant supply of reasonably clean water.

The rapid population expansion of the 19th century aggravated the problem of water pollution in many ways; paradoxically, it was partly improvements in domestic sanitation which aggravated the decline of the Thames. Cesspits may not be the most attractive of human conveniences (in poor areas the contents of the cesspit below the house frequently oozed up through the floorboards), but when properly maintained they were much less of a pollutant than water closets, which began to spread swiftly among the middle classes after about 1830. Cesspits also provided manure for market gardens, and their sudden abolition turned the Thames into a sewer almost overnight.

Curiously enough, the old London Bridge may have helped to control pollution of the Thames in central London before it was demolished. Its close-packed piers acted as something of a tidal barrier, reducing the backwash of industrial pollution from downstream into the drinking water supplies upstream. But the disgusting state of the Thames around the beginning of the Victorian period was probably due more to human causes than industrial pollutants.

Cholera provided a powerful motive for improving hygiene. From 1830 it was practically an endemic disease in London, attacking rich and poor alike, once the water supply was infected, and killing half those who caught it (Prince Albert died, the Prince of Wales survived). The epidemic of 1849 killed 14,000 people, and although no one yet understood the cause of the disease or methods of infection, it became widely recognised that it was connected with bad sanitation.

## The great clean-up

The ultimate answer was a gigantic scheme for providing the whole city with a proper sewerage and drainage system, as reformers like Chadwick had long recommended. This was probably the largest-ever civic undertaking, greater than the railways and, taking the shorter time span into account, greater than the construction of the Underground system.

This mammoth enterprise was begun in 1859 by one of Victorian London's unsung heroes, Joseph Bazalgette: he has a statue on the Embankment, which he also built, but very few of those who pass by know who he was. The whole system was completed by 1875, and comprised 1,300 miles of brick-built sewers ultimately draining into reservoirs 26 miles below London Bridge. The Thames ceased to stink, and there were no more epidemics.

Nevertheless, the condition of the river continued to give cause for concern. Numerous remedies were proposed, and some of them were even carried out, but the general state of the Thames was very poor, if no longer so hazardous to human health. The annual run of smelt (perhaps more valuable than the oft-lamented salmon) did not resume; the river in central London was almost devoid of fish.

The great improvement in the state of the Thames can be dated from the Pippard Report of 1961. Like the atmosphere since the Clean Air Act, the river is today immeasurably cleaner. Some migratory fish have returned and it is possible again to catch roach at Westminster Bridge.

However, a really heavy rainstorm, overloading the system, could still cause at least a temporary reversal of the gains of the past generation. Fortunately floods, which in London's 2,000-year existence have been a much longer-lasting problem than pollution, are now less likely.

## Floods

Floods in London are recorded in the Anglo-Saxon Chronicle, and they have occurred intermittently throughout the centuries since: in 1237 the lawyers in Westminster Great Hall were forced to move about in boats. Over the years various defences by way of walls and embankments were constructed, more especially after the Thames Flood Act of 1879, but without effecting a permanent cure. Several people were drowned in Westminster and Pimlico basements in the flood of 1928, the occasion for another burst of bank building. What finally prompted really comprehensive precautions was the floods of 1953, which claimed 300 lives on eastern and southern coasts. Fortunately they did not reach central London, but they induced shocked contemplation of the horrors resulting if they had.

It had also become evident that the likelihood of serious flooding in London was growing. The sea level is rising (though in 1953 the greenhouse effect did not enter calculations), and London is sinking; moreover, the particular combination of meteorological events which causes the Thames to flood is becoming increasing likely.

A tidal barrier in the Thames estuary was first advocated well over a century ago, and various schemes were proposed at different times. The First World War cut short discussion of a proposal involving a barrier at Gravesend which would have had the effect of turning the stretch of the river between there and London Bridge into a gigantic lock. A somewhat similar scheme in the thirties would have dammed the river at Woolwich, at the same time providing a handy bridge across the top, but that was scotched by the outbreak of the Second World War and productive plans lapsed until the events of 1953. The result was the Thames Barrier at Woolwich, authorised in 1972 and completed ten years later. Unlike earlier proposals, it is not a dam but a series of hydraulic gates, each one weighing over 3,000 tons, which lie on the bottom to allow free passage of shipping and rise to a vertical position to repel a tidal surge.

## Bridges and tunnels

What is convenient in one age may be an obstruction to another, and although the Thames was until the 19th century London's main thoroughfare, it was also, as transport accelerated, London's main obstacle.

London Bridge had been built at the first practical site nearest the sea. By about 1820, when it had been joined by five other bridges (six if you go as far as Putney), there was a pressing need for a crossing farther downstream other than the ferries. This was obviously not so easily accomplished. Apart from the difficulties posed by the gradual expansion of the river and, more

***The Thames Barrier***

important, the unsuitable ground on either bank, there was the problem of access for shipping.

The first plan for a bridge just below the Tower was for a single arch, but this was rejected because of the restricted headroom for ships. The alternative adopted, and authorised by Parliament in 1885, was for a bascule bridge, i.e., a drawbridge, which could be raised to give passage for large ships. The engineer was Sir John Wolfe Barry, and the architect of the familiar Gothic towers which gave the bridge its name was Sir Horace Jones (though he died soon after construction began and the final design is somewhat different from his).

No other bridge has been built downstream of London Bridge (although one is now planned), but if you cannot go *over* a river, you can sometimes go *under* it.

A start was made on a tunnel under the river at Rotherhithe in the first decade of the 19th century by Robert ('the Mole') Vazie, who was succeeded by another ingenious Cornishman, Richard Trevithick, but the work was abandoned after a disastrous collapse. In 1823 Parliament authorised another attempt, and this time the engineer was Marc Isambard Brunel, who had recently patented a tunnelling shield which protected the workmen advancing through earth that proved much softer than the experts had predicted and was, in essentials, the method employed for digging tunnels, including the Channel Tunnel, since then.

Partly as a result of pressure to put commercial interests, in this case speedy construction, before safety, inundations were not avoided. On one occasion Isambard Kingdom Brunel, who took over from his father, plunged into the filthy waters to rescue a workman, and later almost drowned in another accident (soon after he had hosted a banquet inside the tunnel to prove its safety!). The tunnel, between Rotherhithe and Wapping, was finally completed in 1843 – the first underwater tunnel of any size in the world.

Nearly one quarter of a mile long, the tunnel had been intended to take carriages, but costs had so far exceeded the budget that this plan was abandoned; it remained a pedestrian way for twenty years, but then came in very useful for the old East London Railway. It is used today by the Underground (Metropolitan Line, East London section, to New Cross).

The Thames's second tunnel was not built until half a century later, and technology had improved considerably by the time the Blackwall Tunnel was built between Greenwich and Blackwall in the 1890s. Pioneering techniques were employed here too – a new type of tunnelling shield and the use of compressed air. The southbound tunnel was not added until the 1960s.

The Dartford Tunnel is probably the most familiar today. Most of us have been stuck in it. (The 'ford' in Dartford of course does not refer to the Thames but to the River Darent, or Dart, a less adventurous proposition, which was not bridged until the 15th century.) The Dartford Tunnel, which cost £11 million, opened in 1963, having been planned in the thirties but delayed by the war. It is at present an overloaded (hence the projected suspension bridge) link of the London motorway bypass.

## Who owns the Thames?

Until after 1800 Londoners were able to let the river very largely look after itself, but the rapid developments of the 19th century which demanded extensive planning, policy decisions and constructive action, some of it very expensive, raised the interesting question: who owns the river?

The earliest arguments about control of the Thames were usually concerned with fishing rights, since the medieval population was too small for serious conflict over such things as water supply or navigation to arise. As is well known, Magna Carta (1215), signed on an island in the Thames at Runnymede and in modern times fondly regarded as the first step in securing civil liberties for the subjects of the Crown, was more specifically concerned with arguments over who should set eel traps and where.

Traditionally, control of major rivers was a prerogative of the Crown, but in the case of the Thames the City of London maintained rather vague jurisdiction over the river, downstream of Windsor at least, and in spite of numerous minor disputes, the City Corporation's conservancy of the Thames was generally accepted until, in the early 19th century, the declining state of the river and the new demands of navigation, sewerage, etc. brought matters to a head. The government claimed that while the City might administer the Thames, it did not own it, and when the City Corporation objected, brought a suit against it in the Court of Chancery.

The City was finally persuaded to give way, partly no doubt because revenue from the river was declining due to navigation difficulties and the rise of the railways. In 1857 the act was passed which resulted in the setting up of the Thames Conservancy Board, which was given control over the whole navigable river from Wiltshire to the mouth of the Medway.

In 1904 the Metropolitan Water Board took over responsibility for London's water supply, and in 1909 the Port of London Authority was set up to improve the industrially neglected, anarchic state of the docks, taking over control of the tidal river from Teddington to the sea. Then, in 1974, the three organizations, Thames Conservancy, Water Board and P.L.A., came under the overall control of the Thames Water Authority. The creation of this body was a reflection of the importance water supply and drainage generally had assumed relative to the demands of navigation and shipping – the docks having become largely obsolete since the Second World War.

Other organizations also play a part in administering the affairs of the river, notably Trinity House. This institution, which is so old that no one knows when it began (perhaps in King Alfred's time), is in charge of matters connected with pilotage, lighthouses and buoys. The conservancy of the Thames had been first given to the City of London by Richard I in 1197. By the 14th century there were several Trinity Guilds in the main ports, and then in 1514 Henry VIII granted a charter to the 'Guild Fraternity Brotherhood' of Trinity and St Clement in the parish of Deptford. They were given the duties of the defence and pilotage of the Thames and powers to make laws regarding shipping, and in essence, these powers and duties are unchanged.

Another body, less venerable but also remarkably long established, is the River Police. Founded in 1798, and thus antedating the Metropolitan Police by 31 years, they were required to deal with the problem of theft, which had become a major occupation in the overcrowded and ill-organized port of that time. A lively, not to say bruising time they had of it, as is evident from the exhibition in their museum at Wapping. Since 1839 the River Police have been a division of the Met.

**Tower Bridge** c. 1893

**The Pool of London,** *c.* 1900 and today. The Pool of London one hundred years ago was still cluttered with lighters, barges, wherries and other working boats as well as a few larger vessels; but the port has always been mainly confined, as far back as Roman times, to the river below the Tower, sometimes called the Lower Pool. Although there are docks in the Upper Pool, notably Queenhithe Dock above Southwark Bridge, the massive dock-building of the 19th century all took place below Tower Bridge, whose northern

approach road is a continuation of Tower Hill.

Even a generation ago the Pool of London was still quite busy with shipping, but the scene today is very different, both above and below the bridge, where most of the Victorian warehouses have been demolished or converted to other purposes. A more recent museum piece, *HMS Belfast*, a World War II cruiser, is now moored in permanent isolation in the Upper Pool.

Tower Bridge, the only bridge ever built below

London Bridge, is the most famous monument of Victorian London after the Houses of Parliament. It was designed by Sir John Wolfe Barry, engineer, and Sir Horace Jones, architect. Erected between 1886 and 1894, it has bascules which can be raised to allow large ships to pass, rather a rare event these days. The hydraulic machinery, capable of raising the two 1,000-ton bascules in two minutes, was originally steam–driven; electric motors were substituted in 1975. The footbridge, which is about 120 feet above the water at

high tide, was closed to pedestrians in 1910 because it
had proved embarrassingly convenient for suicides.
With suitable precautions, it has recently been
reopened, to the advantage of sighseers as the view of
the City and the river is unsurpassed. Access to the
bridge is via lifts inside the 200-foot Gothic towers,
which are of steel-frame construction, faced with stone.
Originally they provoked criticism because their
massive dimensions dwarfed the Tower of London, but
they have since become a favourite symbol of London.

*The Pool of London* c. 1900

**Greenwich Park,** c. 1946.

*On Thames's banks in silent thought we stood,*
*Where Greenwich smiles upon the silver flood . . .*
wrote Samuel Johnson, the adjective *silver* being a
common one for the Thames though a notably
inaccurate description in more recent times. He also
remarked, adversely, on the quiet solitude of the place
(he preferred the city's hum), and commended
Greenwich as the birthplace of Good Queen Bess.
(The Tudor palace from which she later waved her
hanky to intrepid mariners off to seek the North-West
Passage, and where she is said to have crossed a puddle
on Sir Walter Raleigh's cloak, has long since gone.)

But here is an unusual sight indeed – the sacred
sward of Greenwich Park converted to allotments! The
'Dig for Victory' campaign during the Second World

**Above: *Greenwich Park** c. 1946.* **Below:** *the same view today*

War encouraged the nation to grow as much as possible of its own food, and the most citified folk discovered the joys of vegetable gardening.

The Park is said to be the oldest of London's royal parks, having been enclosed in the 15th century (part of the present brick wall goes back to the reign of James I). The hill is quite steep and not very well suited to the formal layout planned for it by Le Nôtre, better known for work at Versailles. It has been suggested that Le Nôtre, who never visited Greenwich, did not realise it was on a hill. Now, the Park has reverted to grass again, and the Royal Observatory and stone globe have been restored. They are part of the National Maritime Museum, whose main building is Inigo Jones's Queen's House, the uncluttered elegance of which was innovatory in its day.

*Waiting for opening time in Greenwich* c. 1900

**Greenwich Observatory.** It was built for the first Astronomer Royal, John Flamsteed, in the 17th century, and it remained the headquarters of his successors until 1948, when the Royal Observatory itself, in search of clearer skies, moved to Hurstmonceux (the trouble was not so much London smoke as the effect of the street lights reflected from it). Strangely, although when a man is appointed Astronomer Royal he is usually well advanced in years, there have been only eleven of them since Flamsteed.

Greenwich's international fame is due to Greenwich Mean Time and to its position of 0 degrees longitude. This dates from an international conference held in Washington in 1884, which decided on Greenwich in spite of some powerful French lobbying in favour of Paris

**Greenwich riverside,** c. 1936, and today. On the left is the Ship Tavern, the most famous of the once numerous riverside inns, which was the site of the traditional whitebait dinners. These were held every Whit Sunday and usually attended by members of the cabinet, sometimes the prime minister himself. The whitebait would be served, it was said, within an hour of being caught. The last whitebait dinner was held in 1894; the Ship closed not long after and the building was destroyed by bombs in 1941. The site is now occupied by a dry dock containing the clipper *Cutty Sark*, administered by the National Maritime Museum.

The glass dome to the right of the Ship is the entrance to the Greenwich Tunnel under the Thames, which was built for pedestrian use and opened in 1902. It was popular with East Enders taking a day out in the more tranquil environs of Greenwich Park.

Dodd's Wharf and the industrial-residential clutter to the right has all been swept away for new residential or leisure areas.

*Greenwich riverside c. 1936*

***Greenwich riverside*** *today*

**East India Dock Road,** *c.* 1904. The road was built during the Napoleonic wars to convey traffic from the recently opened East India Docks into London, linking up with Commercial Road. It suffered heavy damage during the Second World War.

The tramlines were laid in the early 1870s and, since electric traction was not introduced until 1900, a few horse-drawn trams are still evident here. Trams were more comfortable and cheaper than omnibuses, but the latter had a monopoly in central London which probably saved their bacon. The early trams were American-inspired; they were even equipped with sun blinds, not a vital necessity in London's climate and rather incongruous on such utilitarian vehicles.

By the 70s the derelict docklands of East London had become a potent symbol of the decay of British industries. The closure of the West India and Millwall Docks in 1980 was followed in 1981 by the closure of Royal Victoria and Royal Albert Docks.

In July 1981 the government designated the London Docklands Development Commission as the managing body for the whole area, charged with the task of restoring life to Docklands. In 1982 the Isle of Dogs was designated an enterprise zone in the hope of encouraging investment – by 1988 land values rose to £3 million an acre, with Canary Wharf the major success story.

*East India Dock Road c. 1904*

*Docklands today*

**A Thames shipyard,** c. 1910. A Thames shipyard in the first decade of the 20th century, the remnants of a once proud industry. Thirty of the ships that repelled the Spanish Armada (1588) were Thames-built, and so were eleven of Nelson's fleet at the Battle of Trafalgar (1805). London shipyards continued to prosper up to the 1860s: the yards at Limehouse, Millwall, Rotherhithe and others had a high reputation, and as late as the early 1850s nearly 30 per cent of merchant vessels and more than half the ships of the Royal Navy were built on the Thames. The coming of iron and steam seemed, at first, an advantage to Thames yards, which were able to command the finest engineering

*Thames shipbuilding* c. 1910

skills, and the conversion of the navy from wood and sail to iron and steam, together with the increased business resulting from the Crimean War and the American Civil War, created something of a boom. Even some new yards were started.

In reality, the tide was turning against the Thames shipbuilders, and the apparent solidity of the industry in mid-century was an illusion. When the crash came in 1866 it was so much the sharper for being so long delayed. Within a few months nearly 30,000 shipyard workers were unemployed, and with no real hope of seeing the jobs return.

The basic trouble was that London costs were too high. Coal and iron were more expensive in London than in many other centres, especially in the north, and the old gang-contract system, in which a gang of men

got together and bargained with the employer over a price for the job, was ill-suited to a period of rapid technological change and had been abandoned in all other ports. Wages too were higher in London, due to the power of the shipwrights' union, one of the first unions to stage a successful strike for higher pay.

There was, anyway, no good reason other than tradition why ships should be built in London rather than elsewhere, and the space required by the shipyards could be more profitably utilised by docks and warehouses. By the early 1870s the Thames's contribution to new merchant shipping amounted to only three per cent of the total. The industry did not die altogether, and it continues in a small way to this day, but it was largely restricted to specialised orders, pleasurecraft and repair work.

*Woolwich Ferry* c. 1950

**Woolwich Ferry,** *c.* 1950. Once upon a time hundreds, if not thousands, of ferries carried passengers regularly across the Thames. Of the few that remain, the most substantial is the Woolwich ferry, between Woolwich and Silvertown or, more precisely, North Woolwich, the railway station providing quick connections with the city. The ferry, a free public service, was opened for passengers, vehicles and goods in 1889, soon after the construction of the Royal Docks. It provided a badly needed crossing of the Thames in east London, bereft of bridges. The original ferryboats were paddle steamers. They were replaced by diesel-powered boats by the GLC in the 1960s, when the old wooden, floating landing stages were also scrapped in favour of steel and concrete ramps.

This was, however, a regular ferry crossing from very early times – it is recorded in the 14th century – which is probably the reason for the existence of the old parish of Woolwich on both sides of the river, an unusual feature which was abolished in the reorganization of local government in 1965.

'Apart from the Dockyard and Arsenal', a Victorian directory peremptorily (and untruthfully) states, 'the history of the town is a blank.' The famous Royal Dockyard was built in the early 16th century and closed in 1869; some features of it, including a couple of fine Georgian buildings, add extra interest to the housing estate that now occupies the site. Woolwich's other famous institution (not counting Arsenal Football Club, founded here before it moved to Highbury), the Royal Arsenal, also dates from the Tudor period. It still exists, in a greatly reduced form, with modern housing again occupying its vacated space.

**Woolwich Rotunda.** On Woolwich Common near the Royal Artillery Barracks this rather curious building, known as the Rotunda, catches the eye. It began life as a pavilion in St James's Park, one of the buildings erected in 1814 for a gala laid on by the Prince Regent, with the enthusiastic participation of John Nash, as a commemoration of 100 years of the royal House of Hanover. The occasion also marked the anniversary of the Battle of the Nile (Nelson's victory over the French, 1 August 1798), the latter evoking rather more popular enthusiasm than the former. (Among the other buildings erected for this event was a Chinese pagoda seven storeys high, which was unfortunately set alight by the fireworks and completely destroyed.)

The Rotunda was moved to Woolwich in 1819 and a year or two later Nash more or less rebuilt it to make it a permanent building. Its purpose was (and still is) to house the old guns belonging to the Museum of the Royal Artillery, whose main collection is now to be seen in the magnificent building designed by James Wyatt in 1808 for the Royal Military Academy.

The association of Woolwich with the artillery is probably still its chief popular claim to fame. The Royal Arsenal, though known by that name only since the 19th century, has been in existence since the days when the *Great Harry* was being built in Woolwich dockyards. It was the main centre for arms manufacturing and testing until recent times, but today its acreage is shrinking fast, and instead of the smell of gunpowder, the air is pervaded by more domestic aromas from the new housing estates.

***Woolwich Rotunda,*** *rebuilt 1819*

***Woolwich Rotunda*** *today*

**Dagenham Church Elm Lane,** *c.* 1955, and Civic Centre, *c.* 1958. A little over a century ago Dagenham was described as 'a long straggly village, chiefly of cottages . . . and dirty thatched mud huts'. It was still rural in the early years of this century, and it was not until 1929 when the Ford Motor Company decided to build their gigantic works here that the unemployment problems associated with the early years of the LCC's Becontree rehousing project were ended. Today the Becontree estate houses about ten times as many people as the whole population of Dagenham in 1921. Ford, though the largest, was not the only large industrial arrival, and since the end of the Second

World War more large housing estates have been built.

By about 1960, the approximate date of these photographs, very little was left of the original village, though the live-over shops of Church Elm Lane were scarcely more noble than the scorned cottages they replaced. One survival was the church, with its cheerfully scalloped tower, the result of 19th-century restoration. The Civic Centre, in an unpretentious form of official Art Deco, stands as a symbol of the rise of the industrial community of Dagenham.

Dagenham's association with the River Thames has been mostly uncomfortable, the low-lying marshes to the south of the town having been subject to frequent

flooding. A breach in the old Thames wall during a storm in December 1707 was the original cause of the lake known as Dagenham Breach. After the damage had been made good, at great cost in time and money by one Captain Perry, who had previously been employed in similar work on the Russian River Don, the lake became a favourite spot for East End anglers. A plan to turn it into a gigantic dock foundered in about 1870, apparently through lack of capital, though a much smaller dock was built and is still in use. Since then a large part of Dagenham Breach has been reclaimed, though a pleasant stretch remains between the main Ford works and the railway line.

**Above:** *Dagenham Civic Centre.* **Right:** *Church Elm Lane, Dagenham*

***Dartford High Street*** *today*

***Dartford High Street*** *1907*

**Dartford High Street,** 1907. Like many other towns near the river Dartford owes its name to a ford over a Thames tributary, the Darent or Dart (once famous for its salmon), which flows through the marshes to reach the Thames a little over two miles away. Being so low, between steepish chalk hills known as East Hill and West Hill, the town was liable to flooding. In 1866, after heavy January snow, the river covered the High Street to a depth of three feet; a mark in the church indicates the high-water mark.

A 19th century guidebook described Dartford High Street as 'for the most part commonplace', while the outskirts were 'poor and dirty'. Apart from the church, whose tower is said to have been built in Norman times to defend the ford, the public buildings were 'not of a kind to call for further notice.'

In spite of this unenthusiastic summary, Dartford is a town with a more interesting history than most. It was, for instance, the residence of Wat Tyler and the place where the Peasants' Revolt started, but much of the interest stems from its situation on the Dover Road. It was the first stop for pilgrims travelling from London to Canterbury in the Middle Ages, when nearly every other house was said to have been an inn.

Dartford was still essentially a country town at the end of the 19th century; wild orchids and the Dartford Warbler could be seen by interested inhabitants who cared to stroll across Dartford Heath. But it supported a number of substantial industrial enterprises too, some recent, such as the engineering works, some older, like the paper and gunpowder mills. Bank of England banknotes were also printed here, while the Bull Hotel is a reminder of the monthly cattle market that used to be held in its covered courtyard.

# THE RIVER UPSTREAM

## CHAPTER FOUR

From a boat ascending the Thames from Putney to Hampton, a distance of nearly twenty miles, the surroundings appear green and rural. But this part of the Thames valley is one of the most desirable and therefore expensive residential areas in Britain. Although there are some great open spaces, such as Richmond Park, and some famous views such as that from Richmond Hill, virtually unchanged since the 18th century, this is – now – suburbia.

It is only within the past 150 years that it has become possible for working Londoners to live as far from the centre as this, but centuries ago the rich and powerful, notably the monarchs themselves, settled in this rich valley, where beautiful parkland and woods were praised long before an appreciation of such things became common. Some of their dwellings have survived to this day; a few are still occupied by the heirs of the original owners.

The most famous royal residence on the river, below Windsor, is Hampton Court, built by Cardinal Wolsey and taken over by Henry VIII. Only the Base Court is more or less as Henry knew it, the rear of the palace having been built by Wren as a kind of subdued version of Versailles, and although Hampton Court is still a royal palace, it is no longer a royal residence.

Other royal dwellings, including what must have been the magnificent palace of Sheen (Richmond), have more or less disappeared, but there remain several grand houses of the nobility, such as the spectacular Syon House, home of the Duke of Northumberland, and the Earl of Burlington's Palladian villa, Chiswick House, bought by the borough in 1929; also the mansions of less grand but more famous people, like Horace Walpole's Gothic Strawberry Hill (now part of a teachers' training college) and neoclassical Marble Hill, which was built for a mistress of George II.

Farther away from the river's banks, the neat rows of semis, stucco and red brick, timbered gables and coloured-glass doors, stretch for mile upon mile. The Thames meanwhile proceeds calmly on its way, less than one hundred yards wide and securely confined, most of the way, by embankments, so that it is often out of sight. The desirability of proximity to the river is reflected in house prices, and a sight of the moving waters is very costly. A flat in one of the new riverside blocks (generally more tasteful than most) with a river view can cost nearly half as much again as an identical one on the other side of the block.

## Recreation

Historically the Thames is a working river, and to some extent it still is, especially in its lower reaches. But in the past hundred years or so it has also been a prime source of pleasant recreation.

The coming of the railways virtually ended the river's career as the main carrier of goods to and from the capital, but paradoxically it was also the railways which produced the Thames's modern role as the Londoners' playground. Trains made it possible for people to go on a day's outing from the centre of the city to some agreeable riverside town or village, where boats could be hired and the pressures of city life forgotten for a few hours on the soothing swell of the river. The railway companies themselves soon cottoned on to this opportunity, and the South Western Railway advertised cheap returns to places like Richmond, Hampton or Shepperton. It is no coincidence that the popularity of the annual Henley Regatta and other riverine festivities dates from soon after the acquisition of a local railway station.

By about 1890 the most popular places had become so crowded on a sunny Sunday in summer that those who sought the river for solitude and tranquillity took to venting their frustration in the pages of the press. Steam launches were a particular abomination, as well as bands of overexuberant youths – 'noisy cads' one correspondent called them – of the type which in our day express their yobbishness at sporting fixtures. However, quiet spots could be found if you were prepared to take a little trouble.

Besides the railways, boatyards also prospered from the sudden popu-

***Hampton Court*** *c.1896*

larity of the river. The increased demand for pleasure craft of various kinds outweighed the decline in working boats, and the number of boatyards on the Thames actually increased. Many Thames watermen found new jobs in the boatyards; a number of them seem to have gone into business on their own.

The rise in boat traffic resulted in a new Thames Conservancy Act (1885) giving that body the authority to register pleasure boats on the river and to levy an appropriate charge (two shillings and sixpence for a canoe, up to five pounds for a houseboat). Within five years some 12,000 small craft were registered. Tolls were a useful source of income too and, again, pleasure boats more than compensated for decreasing commercial traffic. Toll receipts from barges fell from £1,779 in 1879 to £1,174 in 1887, but in the same years receipts from pleasure boats rose from £1,647 to £3,805, a net increase of over thirty per cent. Yet the extra expenses were quite small, as the locks, embankments, towpaths and other aids to navigation were already in place; in fact the Thames was in many ways in better shape for boats than it is now. Although some of the locks were too small for comfort, it was still possible, for instance, to tow a boat along the towpath.

A good deal of fun was had by all. It is often said that Thames boating contributed to a more egalitarian spirit, not a prominent characteristic of Victorian society, since the East End baker's family were likely to find themselves bumping gently together in the same lock with some luminary listed in Debrett's. It seems likely that while the former would be in a skiff or a punt, the latter would be, as ever, in a more elevated position in a steam launch or a fancy houseboat, but all the same they were not likely to come into such close contact anywhere else so perhaps there is something in the notion of the Thames as a nursery of democracy.

**Hampton Court,** *c.* 1896, and the same scene today. A paddle boat on the Thames. Sidewheelers were restricted in their movements by their width in the beam, but it is surprising what large boats could – and do – get up and down the river.

Hampton Court was a very popular destination, being about the right distance for a one-day trip. Some came to see the palace, which was opened to the public by Queen Victoria in 1838; others to enjoy the river, the fishing, or the hospitality of the Bell, the Red Lion and the Greyhound. Then there were carnivals, regattas, fancy-dress parties and other entertainments. There was also Hurst Park race course on the Surrey bank, which attracted 'a large and motley assemblage of low betting-men' and where, somewhat earlier, bare-fisted boxing matches took place.

## Romance

It was certainly a nursery of romance. Boating offered one of the rare opportunities among 'respectable' classes for reasonably intimate, relatively unchaperoned contact with the opposite sex; this was probably one reason for the popularity of the river, as it was for the popularity of games like croquet. Young men perhaps felt bolder at the oars, young ladies less convention-bound in a boat. A drawing of the 1880s shows a bunch of girls together in a punt all in straw hats and long dresses, a picture of Victorian rectitude – but there is a bottle of porter in the bow and two of the girls are smoking cheroots.

Sex appeal had its place among the attractions of the numerous regattas and carnivals held on the river, if we can judge by the many descriptions of these events which remark on the prettiness (occasionally otherwise) of the girls. Though on a slightly lower rung of the social ladder than, say, Ascot, Henley was an occasion for female display, and so, descending further down the ladder, were the various less fashionable river events. Of course at Henley the main thing was, or was supposed to be, the racing, but at less pretentious regattas the racing was just one of the sideshows – if it existed at all. 'Sunbury has always been my favourite regatta', wrote an expansive reporter in 1888. 'I cannot exactly explain why, but it is an undoubted fact that the houseboats, boats, fireworks . . . seem better here: whilst the girls appear to have been sent straight from paradise.'

**Walton-on-Thames,** c. 1908, and today. Walton-on-Thames is mentioned in Domesday Book, and a settlement existed much earlier; it is one of the (many) places where Caesar was said to have crossed the Thames during his invasion of Britain.

Much of Walton, especially the centre, has changed beyond recognition in the past thirty or forty years, but this scene on the quay near The Anglers Inn soon after the turn of the century, has changed very little. The Anglers is still a very popular place, especially on Saturday nights, and the neighbouring Swan is also still going.

'The Thames at Walton', remarks one Victorian guidebook, 'is very attractive (with) lovely reaches both up and down the stream.' It was another favourite spot for fishermen, surrendering large pike, roach, dace, chub and barbel. The main trouble with the river at Walton was getting across it. Walton Bridge was first built about 1750; it and its successors have been an almost constant source of trouble.

At another event farther upstream, 'there were no eights, fours, pairs or sculls. It was a regatta without racing . . . What on earth did we all do? Well, we did nothing but eat, drink, and laugh . . .'

The Victorians loved this sort of thing and displayed great ingenuity, effort and powers of organization. Some two hundred boats paraded down the river at dusk at the Hampton 'aquatic sports', illuminated with Chinese lanterns and globes. A band played on a ferryboat decorated with six hundred lights, which was towed from place to place by a steam launch.

Prizes were given for the most strikingly illuminated boats. On Teddington Reach, water carnivals were so popular that they were held every week. There you might see 'a punt decked out as a two-master, with lanterns hanging from the crosstrees of both masts and sporting a funnel, which served to hold the coloured fire . . .' Another punt was 'exceedingly striking with its lines of lanterns twinkling amid a halo of greenery'.

The river itself sometimes dictated the programme. During the drought of 1885 the Thames dried completely at Twickenham, making water sports impossible. Instead, a cricket match was played on the dry river bed, while spectators strolled across to Eel Pie Island for a picnic.

Dress for the river was no less formal than for other venues, as contemporary prints and photographs show. Gentlemen were advised to wear white trousers, white shirt, striped blazer and boater. There was some question whether spats were *de rigueur*. Ladies, in their bustles and peg skirts, their amazing hats, and very often their gloves if not veils as well (the cult of the sun had not yet struck), were even less comfortable. River-oriented newspapers, of which there were many, featured regular articles on fashion.

## Racing

Although rowing rapidly became a secondary object of these upstream regattas, it was a more serious business on the tidal Thames. The most popular competition of the year was the Oxford and Cambridge boat race, the Dark Blues versus the Light. The first University boat race took place at Henley in 1829. It moved to its present course between Putney and Mortlake in 1845 though it was not for another ten years that it became an annual event. Its popularity was extraordinary. It attracted immense crowds to every vantage point on bank or bridge; the start of the race had to be delayed while the course was cleared of a mass of small boats.

The Boat Race is hardly an exciting contest (except perhaps in 1912, when both boats sank), the eventual winner usually being evident within minutes if not seconds of the start. As one newspaper remarked in the 1880s: 'It is not a little remarkable that the declaration of a zealous sympathetic partisanship for one or the other of those learned and reverend academical corporations, the two ancient English universities, should be most frequently uttered by the mouths of babes and sucklings, of servant-maids, errand-boys, and the illiterate streetocracy, who can have no

*The Oxford and Cambridge Boat Race* *1892*

possible reason for partiality to either serene abode of classic studies.' Yet this engagement still retains its popularity, and although the crowds are smaller, national television coverage brings in an even larger audience.

A fantastic variety of craft studded the late Victorian Thames, including Maori dugouts and Arab dhows. The commonest were light skiffs or rowing boats, canoes and punts, which could be hired by the day or the hour. Punts were originally fishing boats, but unlike other small boats, they could, with the addition of cushions, parasols and whatnot, be made very comfortable for lounging about, while the art of punting – quanting, as they would say in Norfolk – although easy enough to be mastered in a short time, requires sufficient skill for men to take pride in their performance.

Punts were slow, silent and sociable. Steam launches had none of those qualities, and although they were not numerous (about 250 were registered in 1888), they caused a lot of talk, nearly all of it critical. The main trouble was the disturbance they caused, which was presumably due more to the drivers than the vessels themselves. Modern nostalgia for the age of steam makes us forget that steam engines were noisy, smelly and very dirty; nevertheless, when one of the surviving steam launches appears on the river today, the considerable attention it attracts is wholly favourable.

Towards the end of the 19th century steam was challenged by electricity, but although electric launches were free of most of the drawbacks of steam vessels, they never became really popular and, along with steam, they were almost wholly ousted by the petrol engine in due course. For all their advantages, especially in relation to the environment, they suffered the same fatal inconvenience as electric cars: the process of charging the batteries took just too long.

**Kingston Bridge,** *c.* 1900. A view from the Hampton Wick side of the bridge, at the end of the 19th century, and the same view today.

For about five hundred years Kingston Bridge was the first bridge over the Thames above London Bridge, which gave the town considerable strategic and commercial importance. It was wooden, and so narrow that a cart proceeding into town had to wait on the approach until the bridge was clear of traffic coming from the opposite direction. Traffic was heavy – 25,000 people, nearly 3,000 vehicles and uncounted livestock crossed it per week in the early 19th century – and the bridge was in frequent need of repair. It was finally replaced by a handsome stone bridge in the 1820s, though inevitably it also proved too narrow and was widened in 1914.

## The houseboat

Without question, the queen of the Victorian Thames was the houseboat, somehow the very quintessence of Victoriana, with its gilt and mahogany panelling, wrought-iron railings and coloured-glass lamps, ferns and flowers, mirrors and knicknacks, brass clocks and birdcages, brocade curtains and velvet upholstery, even, very often, pianos.

The early houseboats – they predated the Victorian era – were converted barges, and although they had to be towed, at first by horses, later by steam launches, they were more mobile than their modern descendants. They would turn up at the regattas, paintwork sparkling, bedecked with flowers (an enterprising Reading florist loaded his stock on a barge so the owners could buy fresh flowers daily without leaving the houseboat). At Henley there might be one hundred of them, though they negotiated some of the locks with difficulty. Although they could be hired, most were privately owned, and guests were lavishly entertained on board. Owners took their servants with them, apparently, for some of these houseboats were enormous, with more room than an average family house today. One famous vessel, the *Satsuma*, with two storeys, had a saloon with a floor area of 750 square feet.

Houseboats of this kind were common on the Thames up to the First World War. After that, though still numerous, they tended to be more modest and less mobile, many of them never moving from their moorings. Today their numbers have shrunk considerably, largely as a result of bureaucratic harassment: councils dislike them because they are anomalies, and property developers sometimes find that they impede their plans. There are still a few, looking a little run-down, at places like Tagg's Island (Hampton), where Fred Karno kept one. On the island itself he built the Karsino, an Edwardian pleasure palace (demolished for a hotel in 1971) where comedians like Charlie Chaplin, George Robey, Bud Flanagan and Max Miller once performed.

## Angling

Boating was not the only recreation offered by the Thames; it also attracted an army of anglers. Although from central London downstream the Thames was practically fishless in the late Victorian period, it was still a great fishing river farther up, and has always remained so. Fishermen were, and on the whole still are, a quiet and amenable section of the population who give little trouble, and so tend to be ignored by the nonfishing population, who regard them as mad but harmless.

In earlier times angling was considered rather a second-rate sport, lacking the manly virtues of hunting. It remained a hopelessly middle-class recreation, practised by lawyers, parsons, occasionally even bishops, but not by the squire of the manor. In the Victorian era things changed; the gentry embraced the sport wholeheartedly. True, they (or some of them) drew a sharp distinction between 'coarse' fishing and 'game' fishing – i.e. fly-fishing for trout – but this distinction was not merely snobbery and the best anglers of the period practised all forms of the sport, like the admirable Francis Francis, correspondent of *The Field*, who lived near the river and is buried near it, at Twickenham. However, in the 19th century the popularity of angling was growing among all classes of the population. With the new awareness of rural pleasures of which the boating craze was one symptom, the image of angling as promulgated by Izaak Walton in *The Compleat Angler* made a powerful appeal.

For many of the new breed of anglers, it was a relatively light-hearted pastime. The fish that probably provided the greatest entertainment was not the trout, not all that common in the Thames even then, nor the famous barbel, whose haunts are today a carefully guarded secret, not even the roach, archetypical fish of slow southern rivers, but a humbler creature altogether – the gudgeon.

**Belt Weir Lock,** Staines, c. 1900. A well-stocked Edwardian picnic is ready to be taken on board. On Sundays the lock would often be jammed solid.

Pound locks, which were first built on the upper Thames in the 17th century, consist of a chamber enclosed by gates in which the water can be raised or lowered to match the level upstream or down, without significantly affecting the general flow.

**Anglers at Kingston,** c. 1890 (right). The technique and tackle of Thames anglers has not changed fundamentally for centuries, and the 'silver' Thames has always been an angler's river, from the days when medieval apprentices used to complain about their unvaried diet of Thames salmon. It still is, though not many serious anglers are to be found as far downstream as this, even now. At the end of the 19th century, although no salmon in its right mind had entered the river in the lifetime of the oldest member of the group in this photograph, prize barbel were caught in the pool above Richmond Bridge. Since the recent improvement in the state of the river, it is possible that they might be caught there again; in fact a number of small barbel have been taken even farther downstream, at Chelsea and Battersea, and one over ten pounds in weight was reportedly caught near Teddington weir in 1973.

## Middlesex and Surrey

The River Thames makes a sharp division in the southwest; the characters of Middlesex (north bank) and Surrey (south bank, with small modern exceptions) are starkly opposed, and it must be admitted that, although, as we have seen, Middlesex has many attractions (if sometimes well hidden), the contrast on the whole is all in favour of Surrey. Nature has stacked the odds: Surrey is wooded and rolling, even quite romantically wild beyond the farthest suburbs, whereas Middlesex is plain and flat.

Like all human habitations, Feltham, famous mainly for its boys' reformatory, has its good points. But it is basically a working-class 'urban district' of no pretensions, and precious few attractions. There are many worse places to live in the world, but it is hard to imagine anyone feeling enthusiastic about the prospect of moving to Feltham in the way that they might if moving, say, to Provence. Still, most of the residents are at least moderately satisfied and probably would not care to live in a place more alluring to tourists. But, as in so many other, similar, outer London suburbs, insufficient care has been taken of Feltham in this century. A less suitable locality for tower blocks of flats, for example, would be hard to imagine. The only thing that can be said in their favour is that they create extraordinary air currents for flying paper aeroplanes.

There is nothing seriously offensive about Feltham today, and it is only when one talks to the older residents, or reads accounts of one, such as the literary vet Buster Lloyd Jones (who predated James Heriot), who lived in Feltham as a child, that one is brought up short. What, one asks, has happened here? Feltham was never beautiful, but it used to be a pleasant if straggly village, with old cottages and shops, a bakery whose yeasty odours perfumed the street and outscented the passing herd of dairy cows, and one or two fine Victorian villas on what passes in Middlesex for a hill. Most of the villagers worked in the orchards and market gardens which formed the setting for the village.

In alphabetically arranged guidebooks of the area, Feltham is followed by Fetcham, a Surrey village less than twelve miles distant as the crow flies. Before the First World War there was no fundamental difference of character to be discerned from descriptions of the two villages, though Fetcham, on the edge of the Downs, has more natural advantages. Today Fetcham is far from being the secluded and (travellers complained) hard-to-find place it used to be; it is now part of the built-up area centred on Leatherhead; but it is still an attractive and villagey place. It is, of course, firmly within the 'stockbroker belt', which Feltham, although it has quicker and easier access to the City, is emphatically not.

**Lambeth riverside,** *c.* 1870. The construction of the Albert Embankment was about to begin. The embankments – Albert, Victoria and Chelsea – were the work of Sir Joseph Bazalgette (1819-90), chief engineer of the Metropolitan Board of Works. Nearly four miles in length altogether, their creation fulfilled plans proposed on many earlier occasions: two schemes had failed to get off the ground in the early part of the 19th century and it took a combination of Victorian energy and the very effective administration of the Metropolitan Board of Works to make this long-overdue improvement a reality.

The clutter of wharves, warehouses and timberyards here were of course swept away. They made room for County Hall (begun before 1910 but not opened – still incomplete – until 1922) and the medical school of St Thomas's Hospital (1871). However, the present view, if current plans for the redevelopment of the area are effected, will itself be changed dramatically in the 1990s. County Hall was built for the L.C.C. and inherited by the G.L.C., but the demise of the latter has made it redundant. The architect, Ralph Knott, whose plan was preferred to that of Sir Edward Lutyens among other famous names, seems never to have built another building of comparable proportions.

**Cheyne Walk,** Chelsea, (overleaf). Cheyne Walk is one of the most famous streets in London, and it has been home to many notable persons. The most famous residents, perhaps, were Thomas and Jane Carlyle, whose house (actually in Cheyne Row, just off Cheyne Walk) is now open to the public.

Although the architectural character of Cheyne Walk has scarcely changed at all in the past one hundred years or so, the environment is very different now, mainly as a result of the construction of the Chelsea Embankment, nearly a mile long, in the 1870s. The Victorian embankments were built over the mudflats, so that space was gained, not lost (they also served to conceal the sewers running beneath them), and Cheyne Walk is now separated from the river by a greater distance than before; in fact for much of its length there is room for a narrow strip of gardens between it and the Embankment. However, what was once the pleasant effect of Sir Joseph Bazalgette's construction is today negated by the thunderous roar of traffic. Carlyle used to like the nautical smells of tar and rope drifting through his windows, and though not everyone did, surely they were less offensive than diesel fumes.

**Below:** *Lambeth riverside* c. 1870. **Above:** *the same view today*

*Cheyne Walk* c. 1890

**Cheyne Walk** *today*

**Danvers Street,** Chelsea, c. 1890. Danvers Street, a typical riverside Chelsea street with 18th-century houses, occupies what was once part of the grounds of Sir Thomas More's house, the name of which is commemorated in Beaufort Street, one block west. Almost opposite is Crosby Hall, part of a 15th-century Bishopsgate mansion which was moved to its present site in 1910 and incorporated with the neo-Tudor hostel of the British Federation of University Women.

Alexander Fleming, discoverer of penicillin, died at 20A Danvers Street in 1955; by a curious coincidence a flat in the same house was occupied by the travel writer, Peter Fleming, who was not related to the physician.

The art shop which stood on this corner in the 1890s is a reminder of Chelsea's strong association with artists in the late 19th century. James McNeill Whistler, Philip Wilson Steer, Frank Brangwyn and Walter Sickert were among the founders of the Chelsea Arts Club, which since 1902 has been located in Old Church Street, parallel to Danvers Street. Chelsea's reputation as a raffish, bohemian sort of place received a boost in the 1960s when many of the most exotic manifestations of that era seemed to originate in the King's Road, but in reality it has long since become such a desirable residential neighbourhood that its inhabitants tend to be rich and conservative.

***Danvers Street*** *today*

***Danvers Street*** *c. 1890*

**Putney High Street,** 1904. Putney is a good example of a village which, developing into a suburb relatively late, was then built up rather quickly in an unplanned way and, not having been redeveloped on any scale since then, is today hard pressed to find solutions for its traffic problems.

Putney Bridge, starting point of the University Boat Race, was rebuilt in the 1880s (the original was a private wooden toll bridge) and has been widened again since, but Putney High Street, which was not outstandingly spacious in the days of horse traffic, is nowadays choked with buses, cars and lorries because it is still, as it was in the Middle Ages (when the river had to be crossed by ferry) part of an important route to the southwest.

On the north bank three major thoroughfares, King's Road, Fulham Road and Fulham Palace Road, converge on Putney Bridge, and the major part of this traffic has to pass up the High Street.

The corollary is, however, that notwithstanding the modern blocks of flats on the flanks of Putney Hill, on the whole Putney retains the pleasant air of a Victorian-Edwardian suburb, substantial, prosperous and overwhelmingly middle-class.

**Kew Gardens,** Palm House, *c.* 1890. The world-famous Royal Botanic Gardens at Kew, which today cover about 300 acres, grew out of a pleasure garden the origins of which are obscure. In the 18th century there were several royal residences here, of which all that remains is the Dutch House, known as Kew Palace. After the death of Frederick, Prince of Wales, in 1851, his widow devoted much of her time to improving the grounds and she founded a small 'botanic garden'. The children of George III were taught 'practical gardening and agriculture' in what is now the Queen's Garden, opened in 1969, a modern reconstruction of a 17th-century garden.

Thanks largely to the work of the famous botanist Sir Joseph Banks, the botanic garden became famous, and in 1841 it was officially handed over to the nation. Since then Kew Gardens have performed a dual role: as a public park and as a high-powered botanical research and conservation institute. The collection of plants that thrives here is more diverse than in any comparable area on earth.

The gardens, the nearest we are ever likely to get to a Garden of Eden, also contain a fascinating variety of buildings, including classical temples, a Chinese pagoda and, perhaps most remarkable of all, several Victorian glasshouses, of which the largest is the Palm House (1848, photographed here about 1890). Built of curved sheets of glass on iron ribs, it is ascribed to Decimus Burton, although several others seem to have had a hand in it. It is one of the most remarkable buildings in Greater London, in some ways more 'advanced' than the Crystal Palace, which was designed several years later, although both buildings derive from Joseph Paxton's glasshouses at Chatsworth. The Palm House, with its high gallery giving a bird's-eye view of trees and plants, was closed for extension renovation in 1984. It reopened briefly in 1988 to give people the chance to see the refurbished building while empty; replanting is now underway and the Palm House is scheduled to reopen permanently in 1990.

***Kew Gardens*** *Palm House 1890*

**Barnes Terrace,** Barnes, (overleaf). The 'village' of Barnes, as residents insist on calling it, is more or less enclosed by a northward loop of the Thames, a large part of the area being occupied by reservoirs and by Barnes Common. Barnes Terrace, running along the riverside is an expensive piece of 'ribbon development' of unusual charm in that it contains houses from the 18th, 19th and 20th centuries. The balconies are a characteristic feature, and found on houses of all ages though the most attractive are those of 18th-century ironwork. The composer, Gustav Holst, lived at No. 20, the poet W. E. Henley (author of 'Under a Stagnant Sky',

an evocation of the Thames) next door at No. 9. Somewhat earlier, when Barnes was a comparatively remote place, cut off by the river on three sides and the wild Common on the other, the playwright Sheridan also lived here for a time. In general Barnes is still favoured by literary and artistic people, including actors.

Despite its river frontage, Barnes has never been a river-orientated village: the relatively unspoiled village centre, complete with green and pond, is reached by following the road around to the right, away from the river.

***Eel Pie Island*** *c. 1890*

***Eel Pie Island*** *today*

**Eel Pie Island,** Twickenham, *c.* 1890. Twickenham parish church (more impressive inside than out) is in the background and an assortment of characteristic Thames boats – punt, skiff and barge – in the foreground.

There appears to be no mystery about the origin of the name Eel Pie Island. In the 18th century Thames fishermen unloaded their catch of eels into tanks at the island, and a local shop (later a pub, then a hotel) made them into pies which acquired a great reputation: there are recipes for eel pie in 18th-century cookbooks, and there was another famous eel-pie house in Islington. The day-trippers cruising up the river to Twickenham on the steamboats lapped up these delicacies.

Islands have funny effects on people, and Eel Pie Island, fairly quiet and residential today, has, like Tagg's Island at Hampton, a history of moderate rowdyism. Before any houses were built it was mainly known to anglers, and in the 19th century it appears to have attracted picnickers, Charles Dickens among them. From the 1920s it gained a reputation for the emission of unconscionably loud popular music, much to the dismay of nearby residents, and in the 1950s the jazz club on the island became quite famous – and even louder. After the jazz club had folded, it became for a time the home of a hippy community, and the river breezes wafted the sweet, sick smell of marihuana to disapproving noses on the banks. Now it is quieter, rather raffish and run-down, like an ageing hippy itself. Plans to replace the footbridge which is its only link with the mainland by a new bridge wide enough for cars have been successfully repulsed, though other plans have surfaced to make Eel Pie Island conform more closely with the standards of Mrs Thatcher's England.

***Kingston Market*** *c. 1889*

***Kingston Market*** *today*

**Kingston Market,** *c.* 1889. Nowadays it contrives to look even older than it did then, thanks to the mock-Tudor facade of the building which for many years housed Boots the Chemist.

Although there is not much evidence of it left, Kingston was an important town in the early Middle Ages, possibly as important as London itself. Several Saxon kings are said to have been crowned in the marketplace, and their alleged coronation stone still exists (outside the Guildhall), although doubts have been cast on its authenticity; in fact, the documentary evidence for those Saxon coronations comes from rather too late a time to be accepted as certain. However, the mere name 'King's town', argues a special connection with Anglo-Saxon royalty.

Kingston, along with (it must be admitted) a number of other English towns, also claims to have invented football – by kicking around the head of a slaughtered Viking (in Derby it is said to have been the skull of a Roman soldier). This event was commemorated in the Kingston Ball Play, a kind of ritual football game preceded by a procession in which footballs were paraded around the town. It was held every Shrove Tuesday until the late 19th century.

Nowadays, the market, which is probably one of the oldest continuing markets in the country, is going strong every day of the week except Sunday. Thursday used to be the traditional market day, and in the late 19th century the biggest trade was not in spinach and satsumas but in corn and cattle. The Italianate market hall, formerly the town hall, was erected in 1840, and in spite of the antiquity of the market itself none of the surrounding buildings seems to be any older.

**Richmond Bridge,** *c.* 1899. The waterfront and bridge at Richmond are seen here from the Middlesex bank. The extensive reconstruction of this area, which had become very dilapidated, by the architect Quinlan Terry, was completed in 1988, in a manner which gave no offence to traditionalists – or to most others. The hint of Tuscany is still discernable.

Richmond Bridge, in Portland stone with pleasing classical balustrade, is a listed building. It is the oldest Thames bridge in Greater London and has fairly obviously influenced some later Thames bridges. Apart from minor changes to the piers, it looks exactly the same now as it did when completed, to a design by James Paine (the premier bridge-builder of his day) in 1977, although it was widened in 1937.

Replacing an ancient horse ferry, the bridge was paid for by a toll (a halfpenny for pedestrians, two shillings and sixpence for a coach and four) into Victorian times. Its steepish slope on either side of the high central arch gives it a proper old-fashioned bridge shape, unlike most modern bridges.

Downstream of the road bridge and out of shot to the left, the railway bridge also has the appearance of relative antiquity; in fact the original iron bridge, constructed by the great railway contractor Thomas Brassey, to a design by Joseph Locke, was built in 1848; it was replaced in steel in 1908 to a design very close to the original.

**Terrace Gardens,** Richmond, *c.* 1899. Richmond has always been a gracious sort of place, with pleasant walks – here in Terrace Gardens, below Richmond Hill – for nannies or mothers to push their prams (more comfy if less convenient than modern baby buggies) while others recline and watch, taking care, in Victorian times, to ward off the harmful rays of the sun.

People used to flock to Richmond on the day coaches, and later the trains, from town, and they still do – you can hear more foreign languages spoken on the street in Richmond than in any comparably distant suburb – although it is just a little difficult, nowadays, to see why. The centre of Richmond does not have a great deal to recommend it, but there is of course, still the Hill (antique shops and a fine view of the Thames), the Park, probably the most natural landscape of any London park, and the Green, with its famous theatre (the present one, now undergoing refurbishment, is late Victorian rococo).

***Richmond Bridge*** *c. 1899*

**Richmond Bridge** today

**New Heston Road** c. 1950

**St. Alban's Church,** Teddington, *c.* 1899. Ascending the river towards Teddington, a high copper-green roof appears above trees and buildings. It is the roof of St Alban's, a building which has become a centre of controversy in recent years. It was originally intended to hold the seat or throne (*cathedra*) of the Bishop of Kingston, and construction began in 1887. But it was never finished: though as this early photograph shows enough *was* completed to make it an outstanding work of Victorian Gothic (the architect was W. Niven). No less than five new churches were built in Teddington in the late 19th century, including the large central church of Sts Peter and Paul which was recently demolished in favour of a new, minuscule structure more suited to our godless times. But St Alban's was never necessary as a church; the parish church of St Mary's is just across the road. Recently, the neglect into which the truncated cathedral had been allowed to fall has aroused strong local criticism.

**Heston,** New Heston Road, *c.* 1950. Heston was a very small place at the beginning of this century, known for the bricks which were made here for developments in other parts, but not much used in Heston itself. Railways had not come near enough to make Heston attractive to Victorian property developers, and it was not until the construction of the Great West Road and the industrial enterprises it spawned that Heston began to expand substantially. The population has grown considerably in the past forty years too, though the scene in New Heston Road has scarcely changed in that time. Craven A cigarettes, which had cork tips to prevent them sticking to your lips but no filter to reduce inhalation of excessive tar, have given way to Marlborough; in general, bill-posting has become more restrained, shops have taken over from houses, and the traffic has grown much heavier. St Leonard's Church, which contains the grave of the botanist and geographer Sir Joseph Banks, is of medieval origin but was rebuilt in the 1860s.

**New Heston Road** today

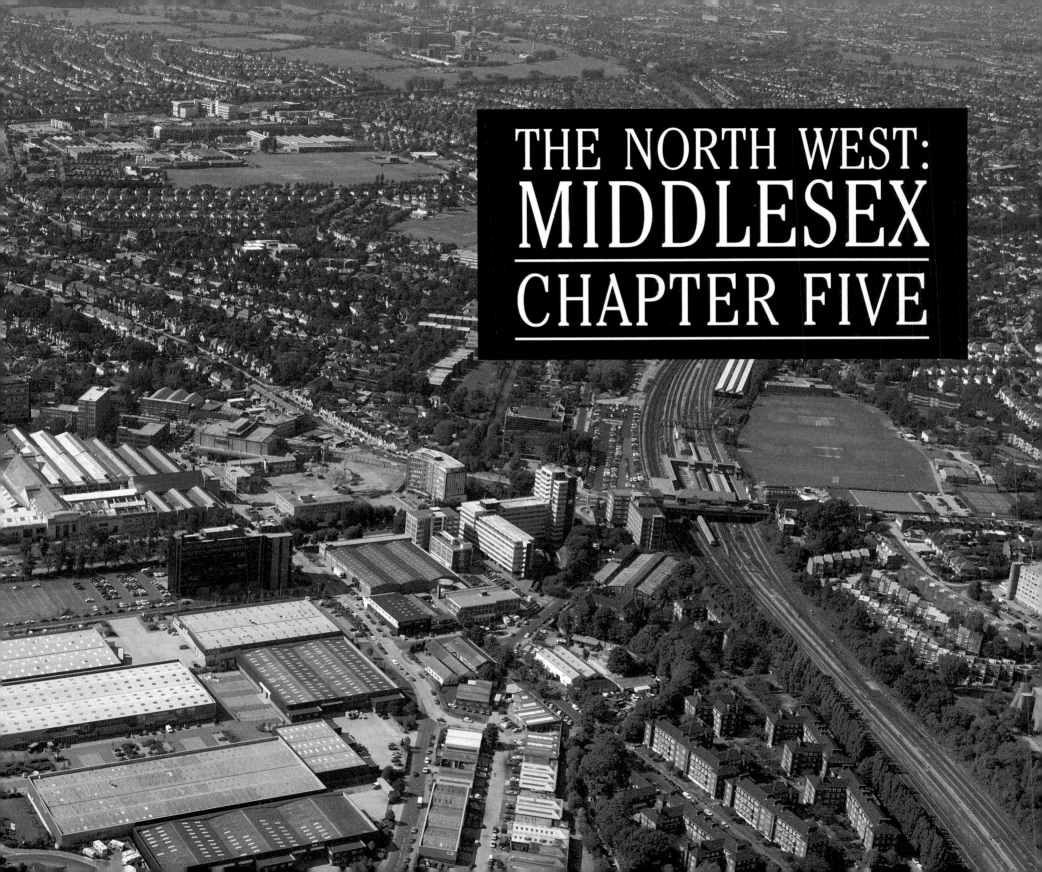

# THE NORTH WEST:
# MIDDLESEX
# CHAPTER FIVE

The county of Middlesex, abolished in 1972, although at only 232 square miles the smallest county in England except for Rutland, encompassed a surprisingly large swathe of Greater London, from the River Thames between Shepperton and Hampton Court in the southwest to the Lea east of Enfield and Edmonton in the northeast. It stretched as far west as the valley of the Colne, beyond Uxbridge, and as far north as South Mimms and Potters Bar beyond the present M25, although the boundary at one time pursued such an irregular course that if a man travelled the short distance from, say, Mill Hill to Cockfosters, he would cross the county line four times.

The extension of Middlesex so far to the east often comes as a surprise. When people think of Middlesex they tend to think of the central section, the 'heart' of the county, lying roughly between the Bath Road (or the M4) and the Edgware Road (or the M1). It is in that segment that we find the archetypical Middlesex suburban towns. Here are Willesden and Wembley, Hayes and Harlington, Harrow and Hillingdon (one curiosity of Middlesex is the preponderance of place names beginning with the letter H).

But what are the features that make these places typical of Middlesex? What is the character of Middlesex itself? What image leaps to the mind's eye when the name is mentioned? What gives Middlesex its distinctiveness?

Once, of course, Middlesex like everywhere else was covered with forest, heath and pasture. It was still rural in the 17th century, when rich City men began to move into the area along with older-established families owning large estates, and in the 18th century too, though the forests were in retreat and much of the land then was occupied by farms and market gardens.

**Hillingdon,** The Parade, *c.* 1950. Although not universal, the most favoured style for the buildings of Metroland that spread over most of Middlesex in the 1920s and 1930s was 'Tudor', here exploited for a shopping 'parade' in Hillingdon. The postwar generation tended to regard the style with the utmost scorn and distaste, but that has long passed and magpie facades are now back in favour once more.

How pleasant to contemplate the emptiness of the roads little more than a generation ago. We have almost forgotten how we, or our parents, when shopping in the 1950s could park the car in the High Street.

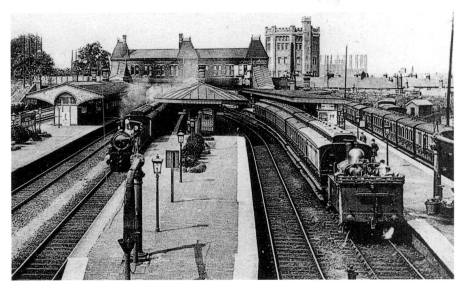

*Southall Station* c. 1905

*Southall Station* today

There was a good deal of industry too, especially brick-making in the valleys of the Colne and other tributaries of the Thames, as well as on the Thames itself. The extraction of raw materials for the construction industry did little for the scenic qualities of Middlesex, much of it a flat and featureless plain. Cobbett, in his *Rural Rides* (1830) in the south of England, avoided the county, which he dismissed as 'bad in soil and villainous in look'.

However, things were soon to change, through the agency of that potent agent for change, the railway. Middlesex had always been dominated by London, in a relationship something like that between servant and master. Middlesex had never, for instance, had a county town, although claims are sometimes made for Brentford in this role. In the 19th century, the London takeover of the county began in earnest. As the railways pushed out across flat fields, settlements sprang up around them; hamlets and villages grew into towns which became mere suburbs. Ancient centres like Enfield or Harrow disappeared in a sea of modern houses. Metroland had arrived.

**Railway expansion**
Someone walking along the Edgware Road from Marble Arch at about the beginning of Queen Victoria's reign would have found himself in open country before he had gone half a mile. Some other main roads to the west were more built up – the Bath Road, for example, almost as far as Hounslow. This was the approximate direction taken by Brunel's Great Western Railway, on its heroic but doomed wide-gauge rails, which opened between Paddington (a rural village a few years earlier) and Bristol in 1841.

Paddington was soon built up, and the villages of Acton and Ealing, Hanwell and Hayes (which according to a local history published in 1861 was a place where 'dirt, ignorance and darkness reign supreme') also began to expand as stations were built in their immediate vicinity.

Growth was steady, but not as rapid as it would become later – Ealing had about 8,000 people in 1841, about 18,000 in 1871 – largely because the Great Western, like the other big railway company in this sector, the London and North-Western, was not primarily interested in suburban traffic. No season tickets were issued before 1851 and workmen living in Ealing had to walk four miles to Shepherd's Bush station because it was the nearest one selling workmen's tickets (in those days rail travellers were not only segregated by carriage but also by train).

By this time, about the middle of the 19th century, it had become all too obvious that the advent of the main railway lines had aggravated the traffic problems of central London. The trouble was that the main railway lines brought passengers only to the edge of the area where most of them wanted to go; the lines had terminated no closer in order to avoid further disturbance of buildings and people, but the upshot was that conditions in the heart of London had deteriorated; the streets were jammed with horse-drawn omnibuses and hackney cabs.

*Bayswater underground station* c. 1868

## Underground railway

The most feasible – the only feasible – solution was an underground railway, linking the main termini north of the river. Running from Paddington to Farringdon Street (soon extended to Moorgate), and opened in 1863, the Metropolitan Railway was the first underground railway anywhere. It remained independent of the large companies it was intended to serve and soon increased its traffic with extensions to Hammersmith, Kensington and Swiss Cottage.

The connection between Paddington and the City made places like Ealing more convenient for commuters. The population, which had doubled between 1841 and 1871, almost trebled in the next generation, reaching 47,000 in 1901. Its fastest rate, however, was still to come.

Other lines, meanwhile, had resulted in rapid building in other districts. The London and North-Western, acting rather out of character, offered fifteen years of free season tickets to property buyers in Harrow in the 1850s, but the scheme, which certainly sounds very generous, foundered on the poor service which the Company, essentially long-distance orientated, offered to commuters. However, the expansion of Willesden Junction, with fast service to the City, was a great spur to suburban development, in spite of the extreme difficulties presented by the original layout of that station, which seemed designed, as one hard-pressed passenger remarked, to test the ingenuity and physical fitness of the travelling public. It was popularly known as 'Bewildering Junction' or 'Wilderness Junction'.

Stranger constructions than Willesden Junction station arose. There was, for instance, the two-and-a-half-mile stretch of line, the West London, better known as 'Mr Punch's Railway', which ran, for reasons many people found obscure, from Willesden to Kensington. According to *Punch*, on the inaugural run there was only one passenger, a solitary winkle-seller, and owing to the obstruction of rival companies, connections were frequently missed, so that the Company was constantly paying refunds on the cost of a post chaise to irritated customers. However, in 1859 a link was made with Clapham Junction, giving the line a *raison d'être* it had hitherto lacked.

In spite of the rapid railway construction, London's spread to the northwest in the second half of the 19th century was steady rather than spectacular. A contemporary remarked that by the mid sixties large residential areas had already grown up around nearly all the railway stations south of the Thames, but 'along the North Western system there was hardly any growth'.

**Shepherd's Bush** Underground station, c. 1900 and (left) Bayswater Station being built. The Central London Railway was the first modern, successful, fully electrified, deep tube railway, and was built with international investment, especially from Germany and the Untied States. It opened between the Bank and Shepherd's Bush in 1900. The photograph shows one of the original locomotives, which were painted crimson, at Shepherd's Bush station. The locomotives were built by General Electric and weighed 43 tons. Each train had seven carriages with seats for 336 passengers, and travelled at about 20 miles per hour. The journey took 35 minutes, four minutes less than the present schedule, and the C.L.R. had a standard fare, 2d, hence its nickname, 'the Tuppenny Tube'.

## Metroland

What was to turn this area into the vast suburban sprawl (the railway company posters described it differently) of Metroland was, chiefly, the Metropolitan and District railways, aided and abetted by the growth of horse-drawn tram services, and later by the switch (on both trams and railways) to electricity.

Most suburban railways expanded on a broad front, fanning out from their original line with various extensions and branch lines, gradually drawing places along an expanding arc into their growing system. The method employed by the Metropolitan was different. From its main, Baker Street base, the Metropolitan Extension travelled outward in a single, extended line to the northwest. It reached Willesden and Harrow in 1880, Pinner in

***Edgware extension*** *1922*

1885, Rickmansworth in 1887, Chesham in 1889, and Aylesbury, nearly forty miles from its starting point, in 1892.

One reason for this unparalleled penetration of the countryside seems to have been that the chairman of the board, Sir Edward Watkin, was also the boss of the Manchester, Sheffield and Lincolnshire Railway, which was in need of a London link. The Metropolitan was intended to provide this, thus becoming a main trunk line (which at one stage it nearly did). Another reason was no doubt the presence of the large railway companies which already encircled London on the north and would have looked askance at an invasion of their territory by the Metropolitan. Unlike its rival, the District, which was expanding on the more orthodox, broad-front system in the southwest, the Metropolitan was, especially at first, dependent on feeder lines from the big trunk railways like the Great Western, which were themselves now becoming more interested in the potential of suburban traffic.

The conflict between rival companies, while it never descended to the pitched battle fought in Binghampton, New York, during the struggle over the Erie Railroad, was prolonged and bitter between the District and the Metropolitan. In a dispute over rights to a siding at South Kensington, the District enforced its claim by running a locomotive into the siding and chaining it down – while keeping the fire alight and steam up. The metropolitan sent in three engines to pull the offender out, but they failed to shift it.

The two companies acted theoretically in co-operation on the Circle Line where, sharing some stations, they went to great lengths to poach each other's customers. Both ended in losing money heavily on what had been expected to be a highly profitable enterprise.

## Electrification

At the end of the 19th century the conditions were right for another burst of speculative building, to house the fast-increasing population, which would be accompanied, indeed facilitated, by new investment in transport. It was also clear that electrification was the likely new impulse in suburban transport: the first electric underground railway had begun operations in 1890 and, in places outside London, trams were also being electrified. The first electric train on the Metropolitan line ran in 1900, though plans initially adopted for the Circle, involving overhead wires, caused concern, bewilderment and suspicion.

In the next few years the whole underground system was virtually revolutionised by the efforts of one man, Charles Tyson Yerkes, described by the historians of London Transport as 'a deft, not to say smart, financier from Chicago'. He was a fixer in the mould of American railway barons such as Jay Gould and Jim Fisk, expert at paper transactions, adept at manipulating stocks and shares; a colourful character, devious, dishonest and successful (he is the thinly disguised central character in Theodore Dreiser's novels, *The Financier*, 1912, and *The Titan*, 1914).

Yerkes, who was active in London for only five years, certainly got things done. His first accession was the Charing Cross, Euston and Hampstead Railway, its line already authorised by Parliament but incomplete. Yerkes's aim was to extend it beyond the authorised termini at Kentish Town and Hampstead because he had observed that although the Finchley Road beyond St John's Wood ran through open country, it was 'very pretty' country, and 'eminently suited for building both the better class of houses and also houses for the labouring classes'.

With capital obtained mainly from American sources, Yerkes next set about the electrification of the Metropolitan and District lines and building three tubes in central London. He succeeded in picking up the bankrupt Baker Street and Waterloo (Bakerloo) for a song. Very rapidly, Yerkes and his associates acquired extensive commitments, for which at the moment they lacked the resources to put into effect. They also found themselves confronted by another great American magnate, none other than J. P. Morgan, whose company had rival plans. Yerkes raised the required capital, though in the process he became involved in financial arrangements of such Byzantine complexity that nobody was quite certain what they entailed, and he fended off Morgan's company by a skilful if unprincipled coup ('greatest rascality and conspiracy I ever heard of' J. P. Morgan complained by cable from New York).

**Swiss Cottage,** *c.* 1912 and as it is today. Swiss Cottage takes its name from a tavern built like a Swiss chalet which was erected near the Junction Road tollgate on the Finchley Road about 1828. Subsequently a bus station and then an underground station on the Metropolitan Line, it was reconstructed in its present form in the 1950s. Sir Basil Spence's impressive library arose across the road in 1964, as part of the Swiss Cottage Centre which also houses an elaborate Sports Complex.

**Barnet Church**, *c.* 1890 and 1970. Through all the changes that have affected London's villages over the years as a result of rebuilding, new construction, road widening, new traffic schemes, improvements (or not) in street lighting or rubbish disposal or what have you, few things remain constant. One that, fortunately, often does, is the single most important building in the place – the parish church. The parish church of St John the Baptist was built in about 1400 and, unusually, the name of its alleged designer, Beauchamp, has been preserved. It was enlarged in 1839, when Barnet was just past the peak of its prosperity as a coaching town.

Barnet owed its rise to its position on the Great North Road, at an appropriate distance from London to be the first main staging post north (William Horne, one of the big London coaching proprietors, regularly kept two hundred of his own horses stabled in Barnet). The railway ended the coaching trade but did not diminish the prosperity of Barnet as a whole, for its hilltop location and allegedly healthful air made it attractive to Londoners.

After further argument and negotiation the electrification of the Metropolitan and District lines began, and the work was largely completed in three or four years. It was a considerable undertaking, most of the track being replaced between one and five a.m., when trains were not running.

## Property speculation

Whatever the reason for the far-flung reach of the Metropolitan, it soon became a prosperous suburban railway and, to the benefit of its shareholders, concentrated on the development of Middlesex and south Buckinghamshire. Property speculation alone justified the existence of the railway, which catered for anyone whose income was steady enough for him to obtain a mortgage on reasonably easy terms. Of course, it had other customers besides the white-collar workers, clerks and tradesmen of the lower middle class. A train left Baker Street at 09.05 'for the convenience of hunting gentlemen', hunters to be boxed at Finchley Road by 09.00.

Electrification, bringing more frequent, more efficient and more comfortable journeys, greatly encouraged suburban settlement, in which the Metropolitan Railway was directly involved: many new houses in Pinner, for example, were built by the Metropolitan Railway Country Estates Ltd.

Eventually, Metroland stretched as far as the beech groves of the Chilterns. The impetus begun by electrification was continued by new lines and, particualrly after 1950, new roads. It is possible to recognise three stages in the development of Metroland moving outwards from London: relatively small terraced and semidetached houses close in; larger semis and detached houses beyond Wembley; relatively large and spacious dwellings at the farthest extreme.

The growth of the Middlesex suburbs was very rapid from the late 19th century. The population of Wembley in 1881 was about 10,000; by 1911 it was 31,000, by 1961 it was 125,000. Harrow rose from less than 50,000 in 1921, to 220,000 in 1951. Trains on the Metropolitan line from Baker Street bound for Harrow, Uxbridge (via the Harrow and Uxbridge branch), Pinner, Rickmansworth, Watford and similar destinations numbered 120 per day in 1901, nearly 300 in 1913, nearly 450 in 1961.

Uxbridge provides a dramatic illustration of the effect of electric rapid-transit systems on population. A busy and popular coaching/market town in the early 19th century, Uxbridge stagnated happily from the late 1830s. Its population registered only a minimal increase in the last two thirds of the century. But in 1905 the electrified Metropolitan Railway and the electric trams which ran to Shepherd's Bush both came to Uxbridge. The population, less than 4,000 in 1901, was over 30,000 by 1931.

## County that never was

As Middlesex disappeared under a sea of houses, its status as a 'county' – a name which still carries an echo of fields and farms, of straw-sucking yokels and fox-hunting squires – became increasingly anomalous. Before the passing of the Local Government Act of 1889, all of London north of the Thames was within the county of Middlesex (except the City of course). The act, which made London a county (an even greater anomaly than Middlesex) and created the metropolitan boroughs within it, left Middlesex severely diminished, about fifty square miles of it having been appropriated by the county of London. The districts which were the responsibility of the new Middlesex County Council were all classed as 'urban districts' and some of them eventually grew big enough to become boroughs themselves. But the writing was already on the wall: in the next reorganization of local government, in 1965, Middlesex disappeared altogether, being absorbed, every brick and slate, by the mammoth of Greater London. The new Greater London Council included reorganized London boroughs whose creation involved some tinkering with old boundaries. For example, Staines and Sunbury, traditionally Middlesex towns, escaped from Greater London's maw by hopping it into Surrey. Potters Bar was included within the redrawn borders of Hertfordshire.

The obliteration of an ancient shire (the earliest documentary reference to Middlesex is 704) caused some distress. But it was not too severe. The general attitude was one of regretful acceptance. There were no protest marches, no bonfires in the streets, no threats of revolution.

Imagine the situation if the same fate had overtaken, say, Kent. What outrage! Surely, the men of Kent – and the Kentish men – would have marched at once on the capital, as they had done so often in the past – and laid siege to County Hall. No doubt an independent Kentish state would have been declared, with frontier posts on the M25 (and no Channel tunnel). No, it would be unthinkable. But for poor old Middlesex . . . After all, there were no famous Middlesex customs and traditions, no local dress or dialect, no trace of fierce chauvinism.

And yet Middlesex has not, as might have been expected, simply disappeared from mind and map, like Phrygia or Cisalpine Gaul. Most people who live today in this nonexistent county, the name of which provokes feebly humorous fantasies in American comedians, describe themselves as living in Middlesex. Many of them also support Middlesex County Cricket; certainly no one has suggested renaming that very successful team, though its headquarters have been in London, not Middlesex, for about one hundred years.

## Acceptable address

The most influential institution involved in this unexpected piece of conservation has been, most surprisingly, the Post Office, that paragon of progress, high technology and administrative reform. So far as the Post Office is concerned, Middlesex is still a perfectly acceptable address (the fact that postal codes should have rendered it obsolete regardless of its administrative nonexistence is neither here nor there, since the same applies to every other county).

Like all English counties, Middlesex has its stately homes, complete with parks, and it also has large areas of open space, some agricultural, thanks to the Green Belt. It has some fine old Georgian houses, though they are none too obvious to the casual passer-by, and medieval churches. Nevertheless, it may fairly be characterised as essentially one great 20th-century suburb. For acre upon acre the interwar semis stretch across the plain: not ugly, not uncomfortable, not inconvenient, but not very exciting either.

People often complain that places are growing too much alike. If you live in Paris or Montreal, you no longer bother to buy your jumpers when visiting London because you have Marks and Spencer at home too. You do not have to go to Dorset to buy Dorset cheese (in fact, if you want proper Dorset cheese, you are as likely to find it in the Dorchester Hotel, Park Lane, as in Dorchester the county town of Dorset). As for architecture, if you work in a typical modern office block, the building offers you no clue to your location. You might be in Edmonton, Middlesex, or you might be in Edmonton, Alberta.

The Middlesex suburbs do have a rather depressing sameness about them. Having been mostly built at about the same time, for the same purpose and the same customers, and very often by the same builder, it

**Near Watford.** *c.* 1920. In spite of the extraordinary spread of residential building to the northwest of London which has gone on in the 20th century, it is far from impossible to find places of rural peace and seclusion, as these young ladies did in the 1920s by a stream near the Middlesex/Hertfordshire border. If these two were to revisit the spot, they would certainly notice one difference: noise. It is very difficult to get away completely from the background noise of 20th-century technology, the distant roar of traffic, anywhere in the south of England, and especially within fifty miles of London. People who wish to make recordings of birdsong get up very early in the morning. That is of course the time when the birds are most likely to be singing, but how fortunate that is, since from daybreak to dusk, the persistant din of machines will take the edge off the harmonious trills of the blackbird.

would be strange if it were otherwise. Nature, where she is evident at all, offers few distinguishing features either. One High Street is much like another, the same names on the shopfronts, and the same sort of shops too. It is only in quite recent years that a noticeable attempt has become evident to introduce some meaningful variety, to echo traditional local features (no matter how insignificant), to consider something more than the barest functional essentials and to resist the slavery of blinkered conceptions of cost-effectiveness.

## The Great West Road

On the whole, industrial buildings have shown more enterprise than domestic ones. While very few of the factories to the north and west of London (or in any other direction) would win top prizes for design, the industrial buildings along the 'golden mile' of the Great West Road, which went up in the same period as those masses of semis round about, have acquired considerable reputation in the half-century since they were built. When one of them, the Firestone building (art-deco Egyptian), was unexpectedly demolished in 1980, it caused a brief but furious public outcry.

Among 20th-century public buildings, distinction is again not a common quality. Some of the schools built by the Middlesex County Council have attracted praise, and there are one or two fine modern town halls, (for instance at Friern Barnet), civic centres, etc. As elsewhere, the tube stations are often the most satisfactory buildings in their immediate area. There are few buildings, including the relatively numerous modern churches, which can compare with the surviving older examples.

To someone driving any distance in the vicinity of, say, Heathrow Airport, the overall impression is not of factories, nor of municipal enterprises or religious institutions, but of houses. In some parts, especially those nearer the centre, the view is of long Victorian terraces in dark red brick; in others, of grisly grey blocks of 1960s flats, where the crime rates are high (and who can wonder); in the greatest number, the dominant type is the 1930ish semi, gabled, gardened and sometimes garaged.

Row upon row of them – but not 'road upon road' or 'street upon street'. There are few 'roads' or 'streets' in the Middlesex suburbs, for 'roads' belong to more open places, and 'streets' belong in towns. One may live in Laburnum Avenue, Laburnum Grove, Laburnum Gardens, Laburnum Crescent or Close or Way, but one is unlikely to live in Laburnum Road, still less in Laburnum Street (there is only one, in East London, compared with seven 'Avenues' and five 'Groves').

**Hampstead Heath,** Spaniards Road, c. 1900. Hampstead, an 18th-century spa, was one of the first true suburbs of London, and perhaps that is why it has retained its character so successfully in the face of modern pressures to develop. As for the preservation of Hampstead Heath itself, London's most valuable and attractive piece of open country, that is something of a miracle as its fate was in the balance for most of the last century.

As London expanded northwards in the early 19th century, the Heath's attractions for residential development were obvious (a tiny part, the Vale of Health, had already been developed in the 18th century). The landowner, Sir Thomas Maryon-Wilson, who lived in quite another part of town, was eager to cash in, but to proceed with his plans he required a private act of parliament permitting enclosure and negating the claims of the local people to grazing rights. Such acts were passed in their hundreds in this period, but this time the Heath Protection Committee, whose members included several Members of Parliament, blocked the application. Guerilla war ensued.

Maryon-Wilson's men carved thousands of tons of building sand out of the Heath, cleared the natural undergrowth and planted rows of willow trees where their employer intended a street should shortly be constructed. But public resistance held up strongly, and the name of Maryon-Wilson was cursed throughout North London. He did not give up either, until death cut short his plans in 1870. His son and heir subsequently sold about 250 acres of the Heath to the Metropolitan Board of Works, and over the next twenty or thirty years more land was acquired, until most of the 800-odd acres of the Heath as it is today were safe (Kenwood House and grounds were added in the 1920s). Nothing could be done to rectify the damage done by the Heath's late proprietor, though groundsmen were allegedly instructed to stroll about scattering gorse seed.

**Hampstead Heath,** c. 1900

*The Spaniards Inn* today

*The Spaniards Inn* c. 1900

**Hampstead,** The Spaniards, *c.* 1900. The bend in the main road by the Spaniards Inn is a famous bottleneck, and the modern descendant of the bollard on the corner of the toll house must have been hit by more motor cars than any comparable obstruction in Greater London. For the past thirty or forty years efforts to widen the road have been successfully resisted.

This famous and romantic inn on Hampstead Heath is said to owe its name to a Spanish community once settled here, perhaps before the original inn was built in the 16th century. Another story relates that the inn was owned by two Spanish brothers, who killed each other in a fight over a woman. In the 18th century it was a resort for highwaymen. Dick Turpin is said to have stabled Black Bess in the toll house (and why not?).

Londoners owe a particular debt of gratitude to the landlord of the Spaniards at the time of the Gordon Riots (1780). A band of rioters called here on their way to set fire to Kenwood House, then the home of their *bête noire*, Lord Mansfield, the Chief Justice. The landlord delayed them by the liberal provision of free beer, while a message was carried to the authorities, and a party of soldiers arrived in time to disarm the rioters.

**Parliament Hill** today

**Parliament Hill,** *c.* 1900. This was the view from Parliament Hill, which lies to the south of Hampstead Heath, at the end of the 19th century. It was purchased for the use of the London public in 1888 at a cost of about £300,000, or roughly £1,000 an acre. No one knows why it was called Parliament Hill, but the name goes back to the 17th century and one explanation is that Guy Fawkes's associates planned to watch Parliament going up in smoke from this vantage point.

Sheep no longer graze on Parliament Hill, where boys come to fly kites and others to enjoy the fresh air and the view.

**Highgate,** the High Street, *c.* 1880 and the Fox and Crown, *c.* 1890 (overleaf). Highgate was certainly a hamlet by the 13th century and in succeeding centuries the village developed as rich merchants built mansions on its pleasant grassy heights. By the 18th century it had become a popular resort of Londoners, appreciative of its clean, fresh air, and was particularly admired by writers and artists. One of its most famous inhabitants was the poet Coleridge, who came in 1816 to stay with a local surgeon Dr Gillman while he tried to break his addiction to opium. A plaque on No 3, The Grove, records his stay until his death in 1834. The High Street

is still lined with small shops and pubs, and in character the village, with its old houses grouped around Pond Square and The Grove, remains remarkably unspoiled.

The Fox and Crown stood near the top of Highgate West Hill. In 1837 there was a near-disaster when the young Queen Victoria's carriage horses bolted. The horses were dragged to a halt by the landlord of the inn and in gratitude he was granted the Royal Arms (seen on the wall in the photograph). The inn was demolished in 1892, but is commemorated in a plaque (inset). The Royal Arms can still be seen in the library at the Highgate Literary and Scientific Institution.

*Parliament Hill* c. 1900

**Stanmore village,** c. 1900. It seems that lace curtains were required even at the pub. Stanmore, in the borough of Harrow, has more history than many other Middlesex suburbs; parts of it are now conservation areas. According to the guidebooks, the name, 'stony mere', derives from a pool which was possibly dug to provide water for a Roman camp on Stanmore Hill. Unfortunately, no trace of a Roman presence has been found, though there was a Roman settlement a couple of miles away at Brockley Hill, traditionally the site of a battle between Caesar's Romans and the Catuvellauni

(now occupied by the Royal National Orthopaedic Hospital). It is said, moreover, that Stanmore Common witnessed the last fight of Boudicca against the Romans. Later, the manor of Stanmore, like so much of this area, belonged to St Alban's Abbey, and Bentley Priory was founded in the 12th century. It disappeared after the Reformation, but a grand house was rebuilt on the site in the 18th century, with a famous circular room designed by Sir John Soane. Queen Adelaide, widow of William IV, died in the house in 1849, and in 1940, during the Battle of Britain, it was the headquarters of

Air Marshal Dowding and Fighter Command. Stanmore thus became a name indelibly associated with the Royal Air Force in its most heroic days, and Fighter Command is still in occupation of the Priory, which in the 18th century was but one of what Daniel Defoe described as 'a great many very beautiful seats of the nobility and gentry'. Another survival, also of ecclesiastical origin, is Canons Park, east of Stanmore, which (unlike the Priory) is now open to the public.

**Below:** *Stanmore* c. *1900.* **Right:** *the same view today*

*Stanmore c. 1906*

**Stanmore,** The Ruins, 1906. As well as its link with the R.A.F., Stanmore has old historical associations with geographical exploration. Scott's companion, Edward Wilson, who died with him in Antarctica in 1912, lived in one of the fine old houses on Stanmore Hill. Another interesting character was Sir John Wolstenholme, whose father, a Lancastrian, settled in Stanmore in the 16th century. Sir John was one of the backers of Hudson's and Baffin's voyages in search of the North-West Passage; hence Wolstenholme Sound, off Baffin Bay, and Cape Wolstenholme, in Hudson's Bay. He died in 1639 and when his tomb was opened in 1870 his body was found to be in a remarkable state of preservation, as if he had been buried in the Arctic.

Sir John was also responsible for building a large redbrick church with a fine tower, which was completed in 1632 and consecrated by Archbishop Laud. By 1845, however, it was in so poor a state that a decision was taken to build a new church. The roof (and contents, naturally) of the old church were removed, and it was allowed to decline into romantic, creeper-covered ruins.

**Harrow-on-the-Hill,** c. 1900. Here is another place with a long and relatively eventful history – it is first mentioned in a charter dated 767. In Domesday Book it records that the manor was held by Archbishop Lanfranc. When most of Middlesex was still covered by dense forest, Harrow-on-the-Hill was the centre and market of a wide area; it included a hunting lodge used by Henry VIII, the site now being occupied by the King's Head hotel, parts of which may belong to the Tudor original. Harrow is very fortunate to have escaped the developers, and now has several conservation areas, with fine buildings dating from the 17th century onwards.

The pleasantly situated church of St Mary, whose spire has been a well-known landmark since the mid 15th century – a rare survival, though the church was heavily restored in the 19th century – was founded by Archbishop Lanfranc in 1087. Of the spire, whose visibility is assisted by the elevation of the site (over 400

**Harrow** today

feet above sea level), Charles II is said to have remarked that it was a very good example of 'the church visible'.

In the church is buried John Lyon, the man who above all others made the name of Harrow famous, by founding Harrow School, as a free grammar school, in 1572. Lyon was a local farmer and obtained a charter for his school from Queen Elizabeth. In the 19th century it became the most famous school for boys in England, after Eton and possibly Winchester (it is barely visible in this photograph through the trees by the church). Former pupils include Lord Byron, Sir Robert Peel, Anthony Trollope, Winston Churchill, who always attended annual get-togethers to sing the old school songs, and many others.

Harrow is now a London borough which includes many neighbouring places like Pinner and Stanmore, all of which became linked in more or less continuous suburbia in the years after the Metropolitan Line reached Harrow.

**Harrow** c. 1900

**Pinner,** High Street, c. 1950. The name of Pinner, like that of Surbiton, is sometimes taken – by those who do not live there – as a kind of symbol of surburbia in general. Pinner *is* suburban, no doubt in the sense that its population before the Metropolitan Line reached it in 1886 was a tiny fraction of what it is at present. However, Pinner, and especially the High Street, is unusually attractive, with old pubs like the Queen's Head, which dates from the 17th century, and the Victory, which is probably older.

Beyond the black-and-white half-timbering stands the church of St John, which though mightily restored dates from the 15th century or earlier. It contains a memorial to Henry James Pye, poet laureate from 1790 to 1813, who is said to have been the worst poet laureate after Alfred Austin. There is also a remarkable monument in the churchyard, of a coffin suspended in midair on a pillar: the deceased had expressed a wish not to be buried underground.

The High Street is the least changed part of Pinner, having been well looked-after since the comfortably off Metrolanders began to settle here in the early years of this century. But it would be a mistake to suppose that all these Tudor-looking buildings are 16th century. On the contrary, many belong to the 20th, but they have been slotted in very tastefully. In the words of architectural journalist, Simon Jenkins, 'This is how Metroland was meant to be. No one should sneer at London's suburbs who has not walked the lanes of Pinner.'

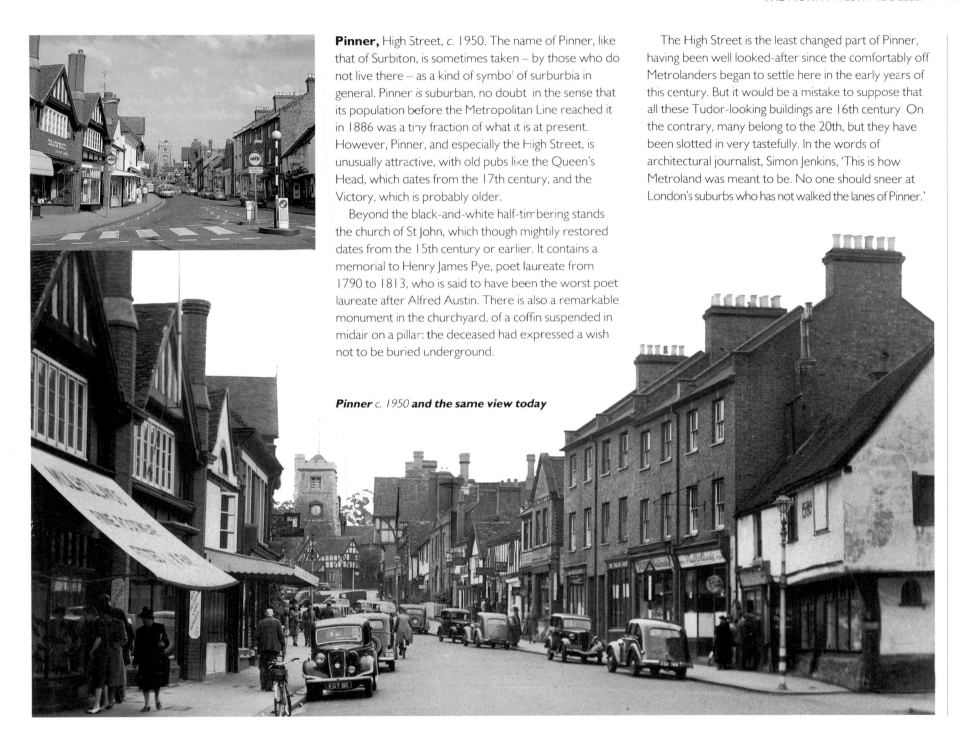

*Pinner c. 1950* **and the same view today**

**Rickmansworth.** Church Street, 1897, and High Street, *c.* 1920. 'The Town is an irregular straggling place of no architectural character, but country-like, not unpicturesque in parts, and pleasant from its surroundings', said a guidebook of the 1870s, when the population of Rickmansworth was given as a little over 5,000. It was a flourishing place – a new town hall had just been finished – a centre of the papermaking industry, with good water transport (not so much the three rivers that come together here as the Grand Junction Canal) and beds of watercress that supplied the London market. It was also the terminus of a branch line of the London and North-Western Railway, from Watford.

The church too had recently been rebuilt, though the tower apparently dates from the 15th century when the manor of Rickmansworth belonged to St Alban's Abbey (the church is also dedicated to St Alban).

Rickmansworth remained a small market town until after the First World War and parts of the centre have not changed much even now, with the redbrick Georgian buildings in the High Street still in good shape, but in the twenties and thirties the town began to spread rapidly along the river valleys and surrounding woodland. Some of the water meadows and woods have been retained as part of London's Green Belt, but Rickmansworth's green spaces have excited marked interest among developers since the completion of the nearby M25.

*Rickmansworth High Street c. 1920*

**Rickmansworth Church Street**
*1897* **and the same view today**

**Watford High Street,** 1921. Straw hats and black stockings, open-topped cars and bicycles with those chainguards that protect the ankles at the cost of rendering the chain quite inaccessible – this was Watford High Street in the summer of 1921. The last of the Royal Docks had just opened in London, an airship had exploded over the Humber, and the first woman had been admitted to the English bar. Watford was about to become a municipal borough and the neo-Gothic mansion of Cassiobury Park, seat of the Earls of Essex, was still standing (it was demolished ten years later).

Although Watford was traditionally a Hertfordshire market town, in the 1920s it was drawn into commuterdom, with an increasing proportion of its inhabitants making the daily return journey to London. Nevertheless, it has retained its own character, and is celebrated in folklore as the place which marks the northern limit of a Londoner's knowledge of the world.

**Borehamwood,** Theobold Street, *c.* 1950. Outside the Crown Inn, Borehamwood, in the 1950s when the name of this south Hertfordshire village had become well known as a result of the film studios.

Near Borehamwood begins that mysterious stream, the Mimmshall brook, which flows north to Water End (near North Mimms) where it disappears underground into the chalk. What happens to it then has never been ascertained. Does it eventually flow into the Lea, like most streams in the area, or does it join the Colne, or does it merely percolate through the chalk to add to the natural reservoir of the London basin?

*Borehamwood* c. 1950

*Borehamwood* today

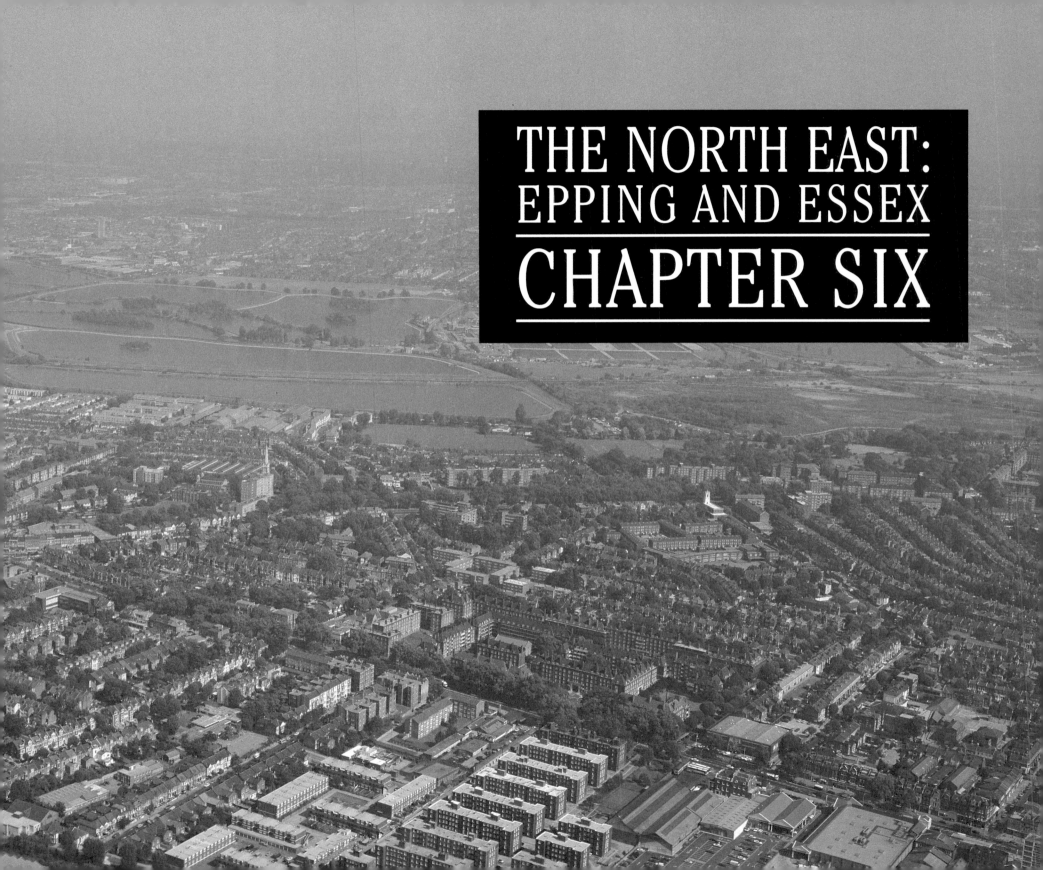

# THE NORTH EAST: EPPING AND ESSEX
# CHAPTER SIX

Victorian London was an extraordinary place, and people were well aware of it at the time. It was acknowledged to be a freakish phenomenon, which seemed to obey no known rules of human society. The rapidity of its growth struck many people as grotesque, even frightening. When would it stop? Contemporaries writing about this feature of Victorian London often used the imagery of seas, tides and floods. London was compared to 'a great hungry sea', flowing ever onward, filling every valley and 'flooding the plains beyond'. The people of London were 'a living tide', a tide which did not ebb, flowing outwards from packed streets to engulf the countryside.

Other aspects of London society engaged the concern of many thinking people. One was the extreme poverty of a large section of the community. The poor in London were perhaps no poorer than their counterparts in the great new industrial cities of the North and Midlands, but nowhere else was there quite such a startling contrast between poor and rich, or to put it another way, between the East End and the West End.

The name 'East End' came into general use only in the last twenty years of the 19th century. It seems to have been adopted as a counterpart to 'West End', which was in use earlier. The name helped to emphasise both the separateness and the dead-end hopelessness of the poorest quarter of the city. For all that Stepney had in common with Belgravia, they might as well have been on different planets.

East and west had been growing apart since the 17th century, and several 19th-century writers remarked on the complete separation of east and west: the one simply did not know how the other half lived – there was practically no contact between them. Writers and reformers were fond of drawing an African contrast: the East End was as little explored as Timbuktu; the plight of an orphan in East London was as bad as that of a black girl in the African jungle (as a matter of fact it was probably worse), but it was difficult to feel kinship with either. The sun which never set on the British Empire, someone remarked, never rose on the dark alleys of east London. The East End, said one of Arthur Morrison's characters was 'a shocking place, where he once went with a curate.'

**Stepney,** *c.* 1918. In Stepney Dr Barnado embarked on his great work for poor children in 1867. By the time of this photograph life in the slums was less precarious, thanks partly to a growing sense of responsibility which resulted in the introduction of benefits such as unemployment insurance. Efforts were also made to provide more housing, though they fell far short of solving the chronic problem of overcrowding.

## Slum life

Miserable though it appeared, and was, slum life had certain compensations. The poor enjoyed a strong sense of community (still very strong in the East End in and after the Blitz, and not quite dead yet in spite of the efforts of the planners) which never existed in places like Belgravia, nor in the suburbs of Essex or Middlesex. Charles Booth, one of the few serious students of late Victorian working-class life, thought that 'the simple natural lives of working-class people' were likely to bring more happiness to them and their children than the artificial existence of the rich. One of Sherlock Holmes's put-downs of Dr Watson was provoked by Watson's remark on the peacefulness of the countryside through which they happened to be passing. Holmes made the chilling retort that no one could hear the scream of a tortured child on an isolated farm, whereas in the city slums at least the drunkard's blows enlisted sympathy for the battered woman. Whatever the dangers of child prostitution, incest and casual violence, the children of the poor were at least spared the savage, ritualistic floggings that were part of the normal curriculum in every public school. Alongside the horror stories of crime, degradation and despair in the East End slums, there are also accounts of warm affection, vitality and excitement. The precise boundaries of the East End were hard to define, and London slums were not, of course, confined to the east. It was just that, there, they were more or less universal.

## Essex

The East End even extended into Essex, in the dockland area of what is now the borough of Newham. Once, Essex had been a Saxon kingdom (and it was then much larger than the modern county) including Middlesex and London. In 1965, when Greater London absorbed the whole of Middlesex, it also swallowed a sizeable chunk of Essex east of the River Lea, the old county boundary.

As in other directions, it was not until the reign of Queen Victoria that London began to encroach seriously on what for centuries had been rural Essex. Nevertheless, parts of the county were becoming Londonised somewhat earlier, in the era of the Napoleonic wars. West Ham and Walthamstow were already sizeable towns by 1820, although Wanstead, East Ham and Chingford were still small villages, with scarcely more than a thousand people each. Yet in the early years of Victoria's reign, the suburbs of London were both more extensive and more industrial in the northeast than in any comparable area. Industrial development was already spreading eastwards across the valley of the Lea, whose character was shortly to change dramatically from the idyllic description given by an angling writer in the 1850s. 'The Lea . . . is navigable from Hertford to Limehouse, and flows through a beautiful pastoral country, adorned with villages and noble mansions, and bordered by sloping hills and woods. No one will wonder at the love our old master, Izaac Walton, had for these rural scenes . . .'

The Lea Navigation formed one of the improvements in transport in this region, augmented by road-building and, more important, railways. The population began to rise sharply, and soon the buildings, both industrial and residential, spread farther north and east. When Greater London was formed in 1965 it took over about six per cent of the area of the county of Essex. That does not sound very much, but it included more than fifty per cent of the county's population.

## The railways

Old patterns of life were shaken up by the rapid development of railways from the late 1930s. The first railways in the region, authorised in 1836, were the Eastern Counties, intended to run from London to Norwich, and the Northern and Eastern, bound for Cambridge. Both companies were seriously underfinanced and their progress was, to say the least, chequered. There

*Hornchurch Village c. 1908*          *Hornchurch today*

*The Owl, Chingford* c. 1903

*The Owl* (rebuilt and resited) today

was no access to the terminus at Shoreditch (Bishopsgate) until 1840 and Norwich was not reached until 1849. The management of Eastern Counties was notably pig-headed; moreover, fares were high and service notoriously poor. Things improved in the 1860s when the company was incorporated in the Great Eastern Railway, and a new terminus was built at Liverpool Street (opened 1874). This proved a great boost to suburban traffic. In spite of the restrictions placed on the terminus, including the narrowing of the eighteen tracks at the platforms to only six just beyond them, Liverpool Street became the busiest station in London. It was still handling more passengers per day in the early 1980s than any other station, including much larger ones such as Waterloo and Victoria.

Parliamentary acts authorising railway construction often contained specific conditions of one kind or another, sometimes welcome, more often not. The Great Eastern was obliged to run a certain number of workmen's trains, and in the event it ran considerably more than the act demanded. This had important effects on the growth of the northeastern suburbs and on their composition – i.e., a high proportion of the working class. The return fare on a workmen's train from Enfield (22 miles) in the 1880s was twopence. The Company was obliged to run only one train on this service every morning but in fact it ran five. As the London County Council reported admiringly: 'The Great Eastern is especially the workmen's London railway – the one above all which appears to welcome him as a desirable customer'.

The result was the first really large migration of working-class people from overcrowded and squalid inner suburbs such as Hackney and Stoke Newington into hitherto rural areas. In places such as Tottenham and Edmonton rows of small, cheap, box-like terraces, chopped off without ceremony wherever the by-laws insisted on a crossing street, spread like a rash. In Enfield and Walthamstow standards were a little higher, but there too the expanding suburban population generally belonged to the lower income brackets.

**Chingford,** The Owl, c. and the new Owl (rebuilt) today. Chingford was suburbanised within living memory. Although the railway reached it in 1873, for the population was under 5,000 in 1901. There were still many farms in the 1920s when, aided by the North Circular Road, light industry made its appearance and the population began to increase. However, today Chingford possesses more of the atmosphere and the actual buildings (such as 'Queen Elizabeth's Hunting Lodge') of its past than most northeastern suburbs. The Owl Inn was on Lippitt's Hill, north of Chingford. The wooden building survived into the 1960s.

*Docklands Light Railway*

By the First World War suburban development had encompassed all these places, but after about 1930 expansion north of Enfield was checked, for a time, by high land values, resulting from intensive horticultural development in the area, which had covered the fields with greenhouses.

## Electrification

In spite of the excellent services enjoyed in some places, it was generally recognised as early as 1900 that transport in northeast London was not up to scratch. The solution was electrification of existing lines and extension of the Underground, in particular the Central Line, terminating at that time no farther east than Liverpool Street. Solutions are often easily visualised, less easily effected, and it was not until the 1930s (by which time the population of the region had increased by about forty per cent while transport facilities remained the same) that the opportunity arose to carry out these improvements. And then, before they had got very far, war broke out and all plans had to be postponed for the duration. The electric tube did not reach its present terminus at Ongar until 1957, and London Transport was never very keen on this line, as little profit was anticipated in the depths of rural Essex. To a certain extent these misgivings were justified, but in any case, within twenty years or so it was not railways but roads, in particular the M11 and, later, the M25, which had the chief effect on transport and therefore on patterns of settlement. (Even now it is sometimes forgotten how drastic the likely effect of improved transportation on land values generally is: the Docklands Light Railway constructed in 1986 sent the price of land from £300,000 an acre to about £2 million in a few weeks.)

Meanwhile, electrification being so costly, at least when weighed against potential profits, an interesting experiment had taken place in the 1920s on the Enfield and Chingford lines. It was known as the Jazz service, apparently because blue and yellow bands were painted on the carriages to denote second and first class. By various devices, such as engine 'spurs' on the track at the end of the platform, the service could process 40,000 passengers an hour at peak times, which was probably a record for a steam-driven suburban service. However, partly due to competition from buses and trams, the Jazz service was closed down in 1926.

## Epping Forest

The present Epping Forest is only a small portion of what it once was; nevertheless, it is reason enough for celebration. Like other wild places, it is only in comparatively recent times that it has come to be cherished. In the early 18th century it was described as:

> ... *a dreary landscape, bushy and forlorn,*
> *Where rogues start up like mushrooms in a morn.*

Persons whose interests were primarily agricultural regarded the forest as a blight on the landscape, and although the environmental importance of the forest to London was mentioned in an official report of the land revenue commission as early as 1793, the Crown itself was among the landowners enclosing parts of the forest in the early 19th century. In 1850 the land commissioners again made warning noises, noting that apart from the growth in malpractices such as deer-stealing and secret logging, the area of the forest had diminished by one third since 1793. Nevertheless, in the very next year Hainault Forest was swiftly cleared before a public campaign could be organized to prevent it.

Efforts to enclose the forest had long encountered fierce resistance from the Essex villagers, who claimed traditional grazing and other rights in the forest, but from mid century they had more powerful allies, including a vociferous lobby in the House of Commons itself which was also active against enclosure in what other wild forests still remained in England, notably the New Forest. What clinched the conservationist victory in Essex was the intrusion of the Corporation of the City of London, which owned a (very small) portion of the forest and headed the fight which led eventually, via the lawcourts, to the Epping Forest Act of 1878. The act, which reversed some previous enclosures as well as preventing new ones, secured over 5,000 acres (subsequently increased somewhat) of Epping Forest for the people of London.

The fact that the Forest has been most often in the news in connection with the concealment of murdered corpses is neither here nor there. In other respects it has remained more or less inviolate (apart from inevitable wear and tear and occasional acts of petty vandalism), whereas elsewhere the advance of the suburbs has continued unabated. After about 1950 land values rose so much that the market gardens could no longer resist, and they retreated farther north into rural Essex and Hertfordshire, hotly pursued by houses.

Meanwhile, the whole Lea Valley had long become heavily industrialised, with many processing companies moving out of London to that area. This also had the effect of reducing the population of commuters: a greater

***Whipps Cross*** *c. 1900*

number of people were able to get work locally, which led to the demise of railway services, particularly in the post-Beeching era.

In other parts of southwest Essex, where the railway services were slower in arriving, less frequent, and less inclined to favour working-class travel, developments were rather different. Woodford, where the main development took place between the wars, was overwhelmingly middle-class. Wanstead also, developing slightly earlier, was a place of relatively large houses. Places such as Ilford and Romford were still country towns before the First World War, though Ilford was in the process of being built up with residential terraces, largely as a result of improving train services (in 1894 there were 36 suburban trains daily from Liverpool Street and Fenchurch Street to Ilford; by 1906, the track having been quadrupled in the meantime, there were 128). Romford benefited similarly, and its population grew from about 20,000 inhabitants in 1921 to nearly 100,000 in the 1950s.

**Chingford Station,** 1882. The Epping Forest Act of 1878 was the culmination of a long legal battle waged by the City Corporation and the villagers of Essex to prevent enclosure of the forest and preserve it for public use. Four years later this happy event received the royal seal of approval when Queen Victoria, during a visit dedicated Epping Forest to the use and enjoyment of the public for all time.

In Victoria's time it was hardly possible to envisage the popularity of the forest (100,000 people arrived on excursion tickets on Whit Monday in 1920), nor the growth of suburban London.

## Rural character

Perhaps because metropolitan Essex possesses, in Epping Forest, a substantial remnant of its ancient rural character, old customs and traditions linger on. Grazing rights in the forest were safeguarded by the act of 1878, and there are still herds of cattle to be seen well inside the boundaries of Greater London.

The old Epping Hunt, in which a tame stag was chased across country by the populace at large (the hunt is the subject of comic verse by Thomas Hood), was finally suppressed in the 1880s, having got rather out of hand, but there are tales of its being revived surreptitiously on subsequent occasions. One or two of the old forest fairs still continue, although they are rather different now, having (for instance) lost all their religious significance and most of their commercial importance.

Some parts of this region display the very worst results of the Industrial

**Romford,** Hare Street. Hare Street is a suburb of Romford, adjoining Gidea Park to the east. It was the home of the landscape artist Humphrey Repton; the site of his house, where he died in 1818, is now occupied by a bank. In this area are some rather distinguished houses, the results of an architectural competition, which were built in the grounds of the ancient manor of Gidea Hall. Hare Street may have an even longer history, as it is likely to have been the site of Roman Durolitum.

Revolution – the Lea Valley for instance, although there has been some improvement there in the past generation. Places once noted for their natural beauty became places noted for their artificial ugliness. Other parts consist mainly of acres of cheap, undistinguished housing, some of the least attractive examples being among the most modern.

Nevertheless, as in other suburban areas (and perhaps more than most), attractive, villagey fragments or individual buildings, often timbered (since Essex has traditionally been well supplied with that material and ill supplied with natural stone), have survived from pre-Victorian times and are today carefully preserved. These remnants may be scarce, apart from pubs and churches, in Newham and Barking, but they are surprisingly numerous in the other, less industrialised, London boroughs (Waltham Forest, Redbridge and Havering) as well as beyond the boundaries, in the counties of Hertfordshire and Essex.

Some survivals are unexpected, like the famous windmill at Upminster, the magnificent Tudor hunting lodge at Chingford, or the 18th-century village stocks on the green at Havering.

There have also been, inevitably, some unfortunate losses, such as Wanstead House (1715), the masterpiece of Colen Campbell, which was demolished in 1824. Bits of it exist elsewhere: some columns from the porch turned up in a Quaker meeting house in West Ham.

Although there are many pleasant reminders of old times, change, not stability, is more characteristic of this part of the world. It is strange to think that little more than a century ago Barking was pre-eminently a fishing port. With a fleet of about 200 vessels and some 1,400 professional fishermen, it was arguably the biggest fishing port in England, and the main supplier to Billingsgate market. The business was highly organised. The main fleet stayed at sea while smaller vessels ferried the catch to port. Fish were kept alive in 'wells', like flooded holds in the centre of the vessels, and once landed they were chilled with ice made in the ice houses on the marshes. But refrigeration and railways worked to the advantage of larger, more distant ports, and by 1900 Barking's fishing boats, like Dagenham's farms, had all but vanished.

Other places have changed more thoroughly and more recently. It is hard to believe that the following remarks about Harlow, today a vast, sprawling 'New Town', were written, or at least published, in the present century: 'A mile of unavoidable high road, terminating in a hill, brought me to Harlow. No sooner had I passed the first two or three houses than the town ended, and there were the green fields beyond. I rubbed my eyes, and thought that Harlow must be further on' (Reginald Beckett, *Romantic Essex*, 1901).

Havering, rescued from relative obscurity as the name of the eastern-most borough of Greater London in 1965, was in earlier centuries a royal 'liberty', with a royal dwelling ('palace' would be overstating it) in the Middle Ages. Queen Elizabeth I was staying at Havering before she went to Tilbury to make her famous patriotic speech before the Armada (an incident recently called into question by historians but too well established in folklore to be disturbed by scholarly pedantry). In more recent times Havering was overshadowed by its neighbours, Romford, still famous for its market, and Hornchurch, which now, however, form part of the borough of Havering.

Little more than a century ago sheep grazed the marshy, flat meadows of Newham, when the gasworks at Beckton (largest in Europe) were built. They gave over one hundred years of service before the North Sea's resources made them redundant in 1976.

**Romford market,** *c.* 1908. Edwardian Romford was a bustling town, and you could say the same today. The recent development of the town centre has not destroyed the atmosphere of the market which is the heart of Romford as it has been since the Middle Ages. The broad street and the profusion of inns signify Romford's former importance as a staging post in coaching days.

At one time there were markets for hogs on Mondays, cattle on Tuesdays and corn on Wednesdays. By mid-Victorian times there was only one market day, but the cattle pens were permanent installations until the market passed into public ownership in the 1890s, and cattle were still bought and sold here until 1958. A description of the goods in the market 120 years ago – 'farm tools and necessaries, clothes, miscellaneous goods, fruit and vegetables' – would do quite well today.

Presiding over the market was and is St Edward's Church (out of shot to the left), a Victorian replacement for the medieval original. The inn next to it (the Cock and Bell), dates from the 15th century and was originally the home of a chantry priest.

**Bow,** 1905. The statue of Gladstone which stood, and still stands, in Bow churchyard in 1905 was erected 23 years earlier, while the great Liberal statesman was still alive. Its original position was in the grounds of the vast Bryant and May match factory, famous as the scene of a successful strike by the female workers in 1888. The church, enlarged in the 15th century, is the only trace left of the medieval village.

Bow, which has a long history as an important crossing point on the River Lea (the name is said to derive from its bow-shaped bridge, whose form is echoed by the modern flyover), was one of the more respectable parts of the East End. It was still little more than a village in the early 19th century and only became absorbed by London after about 1850, when factories like Bryant and May's were set up here. But because of its good connections with the City of London, further improved by the advent of the District Line in 1902, it retained many middle-class commuters.

***Bow*** *c. 1905*

***Bow*** *bridge on the River Lea c. 1830*

**Whitechapel,** 1908 (right). This was morning drill at Myrdle Street girls' school. Up to the end of the 19th century social welfare had depended largely on voluntary organizations, on churches and charities, but it was recognised that education could not be left solely to such institutions, and in 1870 an act was passed to set up education boards charged with setting up board schools in places where no church schools existed. However, elementary schooling did not become compulsory until 1880 and it did not become free until 1891. Thus, one hundred years ago, more than half the children in the East End received virtually no formal education at all, and could not read or write.

The system set up by the act of 1870 was not altogether a success either, because it depended on the capacity of the individual school boards, but in London and some other cities school boards often proved both energetic and imaginative and, besides the basic elementary schools, they managed to set up secondary – mainly technical – education for older children.

**Tottenham High Road,** *c.* 1890. Tottenham High Road, which follows the route of the Roman Ermine Street, was an important highway to the north. In the 1890s carrier's waggons still rumbled in a constant stream over the cobbles. The buildings grew up along it in a haphazard way and in the 1840s complaints were made about unlicensed drinking houses and generally unsalubrious housing conditions.

Somewhat earlier Tottenham had been a relatively prosperous area, though even then well supplied with taverns. Building speeded up after the railway line from Enfield to Liverpool Street was opened in 1872, at first largely working-class housing though by the end of the century a good deal of industrial works were established. The street was also noted for the large number of charitable social institutions, schools, temperance halls, almshouses and the like. Many of the late Victorian buildings, as well as a few from earlier times, one or two perhaps that would have been familiar to Izaak Walton when he stayed in Tottenham to fish the Lea, have survived to the present, and the High Road is today a lively shopping centre, with roadside vegetable stalls and – still – plenty of places of refreshment.

**Crouch End Hill** c. 1890

**Crouch End Hill,** c.1890. Crouch End was a nondescript area then, still partly rural though it had recently begun to be built up and was on the verge of radical change which would make it the effective heart of the old borough of Hornsey (now centred on its prize-winning town hall of 1934). The name 'Crouch' comes from the Latin *crux*: this was a crossroads for important routes which still converge on what is now the Broadway.

The cottages shown here were swept away a few years later as part of the late Victorian development of Crouch End, which made it an important shopping as well as civic centre. The Topsfield shopping parade and the clocktower, for example, now stand on the site of Topsfield Hall, a manor house whose history can be documented in the 14th century.

**Crouch End Hill** today

**Muswell Hill,** Alexandra Palace, *c.* 1960. This much-loved survival of Victorian showmanship was built for the international exhibition of 1862 and reconstructed on its present site after the exhibition closed. It was named after Princess Alexandra, Princess of Wales. Two weeks after it opened in 1873 it was burnt down when a coal fell from a workman's brazier, but it was rebuilt within two years, to a design by J. Johnson, in what was, for the owners, an act of faith. It contained a concert hall with a gigantic organ, a theatre, reading rooms and many other facilities.

The building covered six acres and the park in which it was situated covered nearly 500 acres. Music festivals flower shows, horse and dog shows, bicycle races, archery competitions, cricket and later basketball matches were some of the events staged in the palace or its park, but although it was intended to be a North London counterpart to the Crystal Palace, 'Ally Pally'

**Above:** ***Bandstand Hall, Alexandra Palace*** *c. 1880.* **Below:** ***Alexandra Palace*** *c. 1960*

*Alexandra Palace* today

**Southgate,** *c.* 1960 and as it is today. This fascinating aerial photograph of a – strangely deserted – area of North London (it is Southgate in fact) was taken about 1960: the same view today would not be fundamentally different. What we see here is a fairly typical suburban development of the interwar period. Although the Great Northern Railway instigated development as early as 1871, it was (as in many other places) the electric tube that really changed things in Southgate. The Piccadilly Line extension reached it in 1933 and produced a rash of residential building on hitherto undeveloped land stretching northwest to Cockfosters; it also produced the attractively curved tube and bus station at the centre.

In spite of the rapid suburbanisation of Southgate, which was virtually accomplished within six years, still remaining are some of the grounds of former private estates (as in the foreground here) as well as reminders of the dense woods which once covered the area – such as the coppices in Grovelands Park.

never had quite the same popularity. During the First World War it was occupied by German prisoners-of-war, who relandscaped the park, and in 1936 part of it was acquired by the BBC as a studio from which the world's first public television broadcast was made.

After the Second World War it became rather scruffy. A guidebook described it in 1970 as a 'huge sluggish building . . . standing in a blowsy litter-ridden park, part of which is now used as a car auction meeting place'. In July 1980 it caught fire again and was almost completely gutted. This calamity had the effect of arousing hitherto unsuspected affection for the building, which ensured its reconstruction. Rather lavish plans were made for the restored building, which had undeniably become something of a white elephant. The main exhibition hall reopened in March 1988, by which time the actual fire damage had been rectified although further reconstruction was still going on. Today, its restoration is complete.

*Southgate* c. 1960

**Walthamstow,** St Mary's Church, c. 1919. Walthamstow, now a constituent part of the borough of Waltham Forest, is a very old place. A Bronze Age oak canoe, found when the reservoirs were being built in Walthamstow Marshes at the beginning of this century, is now in the British Museum. In King Alfred's time the Danes were defeated here when the River Lea was temporarily blocked by the crafty Saxons lower down, leaving the Danish fort on Mersea Island high and dry.

Guarded by the Lea and the expanse of the marshes on one side and by forest on the other, Walthamstow remained a smallish village until comparatively recent times, despite a few industrial developments such as the copper mill (the building still exists) which was in operation about the time of the battle of Trafalgar. It was one of a number of small agricultural settlements in this region, and traces of this former character can still be seen around St Mary's Church.

*Walthamstow c. 1919*

*Walthamstow today*

It was popular with City merchants from the late 17th century, but at the beginning of the 19th the population of Walthamstow was only about 3,000. By 1850 it had not risen above 5,000, although the railway had reached Lea Bridge in 1840. It was not until the Chingford line was built right through the centre of Walthamstow about 30 years later that development took off. By 1900 the population was approaching 100,000. The North Circular Road provided further stimulus in the 1920s and 1930s, but Walthamstow suffered heavy bomb damage during the Second World War, with the result that the most prominent buildings today are tower blocks and shopping precincts.

The picturesque remnants of old Walthamstow are now, of course, carefully preserved, and Waltham Forest Council adheres to the belief of one of Walthamstow's most famous citizens, William Morris, that fine old buildings 'are not in any sense our own property . . . We are only trustees . . .'

**Woodford Green** c. 1920

**Woodford Green** today

**Woodford Green,** c. 1920 and today. Woodford was original y a village in the middle of the forest, but from the 17th century it attracted wealthy City men, a few of whose large houses survive, though no longer in private ownership. Harts, which is now a hospital, was once owned by a famous 18th-century botanist, Richard Warner, who originated the cultivation of gardenias in England.

With the arrival of the railway the various Woodford parishes became suburbs, the old private estates being carved up for new streets and houses, although the fastest growth occurred in this century. Woodford is unusual in northeast London for its high proportion of commodious, upper-middle-class, detached houses, which is largely the result of relatively poor train service and, in particular, the absence of workmen's trains. Some compensation for this neglect of the labouring classes may be sensed in the imposing proportions of the Woodford Working Men's Club, with its domed clocktower, built in 1906 and just visible towards the end of the High Road.

**Upminster,** c. 1909 (overleaf). When the east-bound traveller reaches Upminster, he may feel that at last he is in sight of rural Essex. Although Upminster can be reached – since 1932 – on the District Line, and has now been drawn into the urban orbit of Romford and Hornchurch, it is still rural in parts, though not quite so charmingly pastoral as is suggested by this photograph of Bird's Lane Corner in about 1910. Upminster still has its medieval tithe barn, a 16th-century farmhouse, its famous smock windmill, built in 1803 and recently restored to working order, as well as a number of other old listed buildings – Upminster Hall, partly Tudor, has become the club house of the Upminster Golf Club. The church is also famous. From its tower, below the unusual spire, Dr William Derham, rector in the early 18th century, calculated the speed of sound by comparing the sight and sound of gunfire from Woolwich Arsenal.

**Upminster** c. 1909

**Upminster** today

**Ilford,** *c.* 1939. An entrance to the subway and Gants Hill Underground station, north Ilford, looking north towards Woodford Avenue. To the south is the attractive and extensive Valentines Park, once the estate belonging to a still extant mansion which was originally built in the 1690s. It now houses offices of Redbridge Borough Council, a familiar fate for such buildings (and as Hermione Gingold said to Noel Coward when he complained of being seventy, 'Better than the alternative'). The house was famous for its great vine, planted in 1758, which stretched two hundred feet along the south wall and provided the cutting (in 1760) from which was grown the even more famous vine at Hampton Court. The latter is still flourishing, but its parent perished in 1875 when a new gardener, tidying up, uprooted it and threw it on a bonfire.

The railway reached Ilford comparatively early – in 1839 – although its fastest growth occurred in this century. At the census of 1891 the population was about 11,000; by the 1950s it was 180,000. Like so much of northeast London, it consists today largely of well-kept housing estates without much to distinguish them architecturally from others of the same vintage.

*Ilford, Gants Hill Station c. 1939*

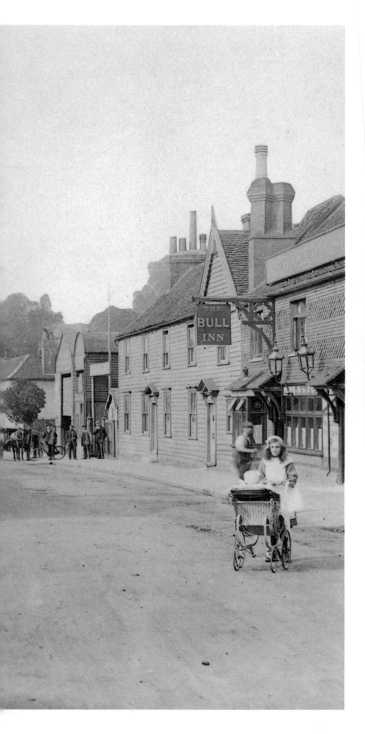

**Left:** *Hornchurch* c. *1919* and **Above:** *the same view today*

**Hornchurch,** c. 1919 and 1909 (overleaf). Hornchurch is today a quieter place than Romford, and is even less certainly a part of Greater London. Less than one hundred years ago it was a quiet village and it still has a country air in parts, even if the High Street now looks entirely different from the village street of of about 70 years ago when these photographs were taken. There is still a Bull Inn and it still serves the local ale, but it's a very different house from the tile-clad pub of Edwardian times, having been most recently rebuilt about 1950. Nor do the Hornchurch butchers nowadays hang their meat in the open air to attract passing flies, flying mud or schoolboy's missiles. The wooden buildings seen here lasted until after the Second World War but were pulled down during redevelopment a few years later leaving only the King's Head and the three 17th century buildings above. Beside the church is the Dell (see overleaf) once used for fairs and other public entertainments.

The corner of North Street and the High Street is also unfamiliar, only the Baptist Chapel surviving as a landmark. The stucco building on the corner was the Britannia Inn, later used as parish council offices.

The famous R.A.F. airfield south of Hornchurch, the scene of almost legendary exploits in 1940, was sold for building land in the 1960s.

**Hornchurch,** *The Dell 1909*

*Loughton* 1923

**Loughton,** 1923. The newly erected war memorial stands in front of the King's Head Hotel which had itself been rebuilt not long before. Loughton was the main point of entry for visitors to Epping Forest (hence, no doubt, the profusion of 'tea rooms'), and Loughton villagers had been in the forefront of the battle to save Epping Forest from enclosure.

There is something sadly ironic about the presence in nearly every English parish of a memorial, often elaborate and expensive, to those killed in the First World War. Naturally, nobody thought of leaving room for the names of those who were to be killed in the next war, although as things turned out that was less than twenty years away. Their names were squeezed in somehow; admittedly, there were less of them than in 1914-19 and, after all, one could hardly erect a second monument like the first.

*Loughton* today

# THE SOUTH EAST:
## DOWNE TO DULWICH
# CHAPTER SEVEN

Except along the river and in Southwark, London scarcely encroached on the country south of the River Thames until the 19th century. Eighteenth-century Camberwell, for instance, was a small village surrounded by fields, famous for its orchards and gardens, where in summer the Camberwell Beauty butterfly could still be seen. Lewisham was a place of working farms and large estates. Catford was a rather depressed agricultural village hampered by sodden soil and flooding. Dulwich was difficult to reach from town, and wise persons did not travel thither alone or unarmed.

Dulwich is, in its way, unique. If the objective of a suburb is to remain as antiquely rural as possible and to deny the existence of its city connections, then Dulwich is a paragon. No other London suburb has been so successful in preserving its village-like atmosphere and appearance. The centre of Dulwich, once simply the High Street, is officially called Dulwich Village,

the village itself a hamlet. Every guidebook pays tribute to this arcadian character; every inhabitant bears witness to it. In the end one can grow rather tired of it and may have to fight down an impulse to spray-paint graffiti on the quaint old tollgate or scatter lager cans around the Park. In any case, the Village is only part of Dulwich, which also has much unpretentious middle- and lower-class housing and in East Dulwich a rather poor and shabby district.

## Alleyn's influence

The manor of Dulwich, which was in monastic hands until Henry VIII's Dissolution, was purchased in the early years of the 17th century by the prosperous actor, Edward Alleyn. Having no children himself, he invested the money he had made as a bear-baiting impresario in a school, together with alms houses and a chapel. Like many other educational institutions of

**Dulwich College** today

**Tooting Bec** is mentioned in Domesday Book as being held by the Benedictine Abbey of St Mary of Bec in Normandy. By the 18th century it had become a fashionable place to have a country residence, and several large mansions were built around the Common. Streatham Park was the home of the Thrales, near the south side of the Common, and Dr Johnson was a frequent visitor.

ancient foundation, the school was founded for poor boys only to become in course of time a school for the sons of the rich. However, even in the complacent 18th century, Dulwich College never quite forgot its charitable duties. When John Evelyn visited it some fifty years after the death of its founder, he reported: 'I went to see Dulwich College, being the pious foundation of one Allen, a famous comedian in King James's time. The Chapell is pretty, the rest of the Hospital was very ill contrived [it *was* badly built: one wing had collapsed some years before Evelyn's visit], yet it maintains divers poore of both sexes. 'Tis in a melancholy part of Cam[b]erwell parish.'

Since the 17th century the history of Dulwich has been closely linked with the College of God's Gift (to give it its proper name) and the influence of Alleyn's foundation, which kept the medieval manor intact down to the present, has been primarily responsible for the modern character of the place.

## South London spa

Dulwich first acquired some fame among Londoners in the same way as Hampstead, of which in many ways it is a south London counterpart, and that was as a 'spa' – a role that could be and usually was adopted by any halfway respectable place with freshwater springs. Dulwich Wells, the 18th-century spa, was on the east side of Dulwich Park. Visitors took their repast at the Green Man, which stood where the Grove Tavern is now, and a few wealthy people built houses in Dulwich, although the College insisted on relatively short (21 years) leases. Some of these houses are still standing. They include Lydenhurst, Bell House and some other Georgian houses in Dulwich Village, though it is extremely difficult to distinguish the modern reproductions from the genuine article.

Another 18th-century innovation was the Dulwich Dining Club, formed in the 1780s for the mutual entertainment of the prosperous new residents. Originally intended, a local historian reports, as 'an excuse for an annual dinner when the gentlemen of Dulwich could escape from the ladies and drink themselves under the table', it has evolved over the years, and its contemporary descendant is called the Dulwich Working Men's Club, which was established in the 1930s and whose members are predominantly female!

The amenities of Dulwich were greatly advanced early in the 19th century by the foundation of Dulwich Picture Gallery, the first public art gallery in England, though at first members of the public were admitted only on one day in the week. The Gallery helped to make Dulwich a popular place for excursions from 'the smoke', as a new road had improved its notoriously poor communications with the capital. In the same period Dulwich College gained the right to enclose parts of the Common, which added greatly to its financial resources, especially with the advent of the railways and the concomitant demand for building land.

## Railways

However, in Dulwich railways were not regarded with universal approval. Ruskin, who had once gathered hawthorn buds with his mother in Croxted Lane (Road) and later wandered by himself from his house in Herne Hill among Dulwich's arbours, ruminating on modern painters, deplored the ruination of what he called the 'once-lovely fields of Dulwich' by the crowds of railway-borne visitors to the Crystal Palace – transferred to Sydenham in 1854 and swiftly followed there by the railway.

The College governors, in spite of the potential financial gains, did not care for the railways either. For some time they resisted the encroachment of

***London Bridge*** *c. 1860*

the London, Chatham and Dover Railway Company, and they also insisted that railway bridges in Dulwich should be in cast iron and designed by Charles Barry, who at the time (in the 1860s) was employed on the rebuilding of the College. His imposing yet decorative buildings, separated from what is now the congested South Circular Road by lawns of intense green, were finished in 1870.

At that date there were still only about 700 houses in Dulwich, but the railways inevitably brought extensive development. The population, which had been less than 2,000 in 1851, rose to over 10,000 by 1901. The view from Dog Kennel Hill towards Sydenham, much admired fifty years before as a stretch of mixed woodland inhabited by gypsies, changed completely. What Walter Besant saw in about 1900 was a 'deadly monotony of row upon row of identical houses'.

In East Dulwich, beyond the preserves of the College governors and built up almost entirely in the last quarter of the 19th century, the builders went to some effort to introduce variety, including unnecessary twists and turns in the streets as well as a selection of 'artistic' extras on gables, windows and doorways. These efforts, which by now have gained a certain charm (though not the kind that's called irresistible), can be explained by a temporary lull in the market for lower-middle-class suburban housing at the time when East Dulwich was developed.

## Suburban services

Suburban railway services came early to southeast London, which partly explains why there are practically no Underground lines in that region. The oldest of London's main railway termini is London Bridge, which started life in 1836 as two wooden platforms and a gate, serving the London and Greenwich Railway. A viaduct was built across much of the grisliest part of Bermondsey, where no custom was to be expected, and the Company recouped some of its investment by letting the spaces under the arches as shops, warehouses, even homes (in the Second World War the railway arches made useful air-raid shelters). Soon the station had to be expanded, as half a dozen different companies (soon amalgamated, however) began to use it, and London Bridge was linked up with Charing Cross, Waterloo and Victoria. The South-Eastern Railway, in an effort to circumvent the London and Greenwich (which it afterwards absorbed), opened Bricklayer's Arms in 1844, but it was not a success as a passenger station and was soon turned over to freight exclusively (it was closed altogether in 1981). In 1846 some 625,000 passengers passed through London Bridge station; in eight years the number has risen to 10,800,000.

In spite of excursions to Crystal Palace and other destinations, London Bridge was a working people's station, with traffic concentrated heavily in the rush hours. This is still the case today, just as Victoria has always been the main centre for holiday traffic, with the swift and frequent Gatwick Airport service now added to its traditional links with the continent and the south coast.

Difficulties were often caused when changing custom affected railway traffic. For example, Cannon Street Station, with eight platforms, used to be busier than Charing Cross, with six. In 1927 Cannon Street had 213 suburban trains a day, whereas Charing Cross had 206. But during the next ten years increasing travel between the suburbs and the West End made Charing Cross the more popular station: it then had 338 suburban trains a day whereas Cannon Street traffic was almost unchanged with 220. But – Cannon Street still had two more platforms than Charing Cross!

**Caterham,** Waller Lane, c. 1903. Although this photograph seems to have been taken on a weekday the little girls on the right, carrying posies and wearing sensational hats, are presumably on their way from church. On the opposite side of the street, renegades.

The Church is St John's, Caterham Valley, and was built in the 1880s for what was then a comparatively new parish of, largely, commuters. The old village, once quite separate, is Caterham-on-the-Hill.

## Housing density

Up to about 1950 housing density in a place such as Orpington, a very far-flung suburb, was remarkably low – about three houses per acre (in Bexley, also largely developed in the 20th century, it was over 18 per acre but that was still not a very high density). A study of the growth of the built-up area between the world wars makes it immediately obvious how influential was the electrification of the railways (and also trams to some extent) in the 1920s. It was this that made it possible for people to move farther away into low-density housing areas, where the advertisements of property for sale invariably made much of the proximity to the electric line.

Electrification produced a marked rise, naturally, in railway passengers, especially in those buying season tickets. For example, season ticket sales at Beckenham Junction rose from 5,345 in 1927 to 14,680 in 1934. The rise at Orpington for the same years was 2,677 to 13,378. West Wickham, built up comparatively late, showed an even more dramatic rise, from 336 in 1925 to 18,711 in 1934.

*Caterham Waller Lane* 1903

## Blackheath

The history of Dulwich is of course exceptional, but Dulwich shares with other places in the southeast a history of comparatively early suburban development, due mainly to the railway network established by about the middle of the 19th century, which was so extensive that, to this day, southeast London and adjacent parts of Kent are largely ignored by the Underground, which ventures no farther than New Cross. Another place, with an even older (and much more rumbustious) history than Dulwich which today strives hard to maintain its 'village' status is Blackheath.

The name is rather grim; it is probably a corruption of Black Heath, which is even grimmer. On the flat and windy heath, later a favourite resort of highwaymen (hence Shooters Hill), Wat Tyler's followers assembled in 1381 before marching on London, where a bloodbath is said to have been avoided by the quick wit of a youthful Richard II. Later, Jack Cade's rebels marshalled there, but it was not only Kentish rebels who assembled on Blackheath – Henry VII slaughtered some disgruntled Cornishmen on the heath – and it was also a meeting place on other, more amiable occasions, such as the Londoners' welcome to King Charles II on his return to power in 1660, or the meetings of revivalist preachers like Wesley and Whitefield in the 18th century. The fair, still held every year, is not a very ancient tradition as fairs go, but Blackheath was a pioneer of popular modern sporting contests, site of the first golf club in England (the date is disputed) and also of the first Rugby football club (1862).

Blackheath is only six miles from London and on an ancient and well-travelled highway, so it is not surprising that a residential suburb began to develop as early as the late 18th century. Some houses of that period can still be seen around the heath, which is somewhat diminished since then. It was not improved by extensive gravel digging in the 19th century, which was only stopped when the Metropolitan Commons Act was passed in 1866, securing 267 acres of the heath for the public's benefit.

What is now known as Blackheath Village (with its pleasantly named addition of Tranquil Vale) is relatively modern. It was virtually non-existent at the end of the 18th century and did not become a real community until the boom of the 1840s and 1850s, associated with the advent of the railway. Some fine solid houses were built at this time, many of which still exist though now divided into flats. The Village received a church, All Saints, in

1859, and within about twenty years there were four other churches or chapels in Blackheath (not all postdating All Saints). A famous inn, the Green Man, the name of which survives though the pub itself has gone, had a hall where various kinds of entertainment were put on before Alexandra Hall (today a bank) was built. There was a skating rink which served also as a lecture hall (Stanley appeared there to relate his African adventures) and, despite the noisy proximity of the railway, as a recital hall.

Victorian Blackheath was altogether a lively community, strong on intellectual and artistic interests. The Conservatoire of Music is still going but the Art School foundered during the First World War – a casualty of either the Modern Movement or the wartime policy. Education was a powerful force in Blackheath, which had a bewildering number of schools in the 19th century, some very small and short-lived. Benjamin Disraeli went to one of them until the age of thirteen; it was run by a Non-conformist minister and ran to a visiting teacher in Hebrew. More notable establishments included Blackheath High School for Girls, founded in 1880, something of a pioneer in girls' secondary education and what is now Eltham College, originally founded in Blackheath as a school for the sons of missionaries of 1857.

## Beckenham

As the railway moved farther into Kent it sucked in more distant villages to suburbia. Beckenham, for instance, was described in the 1870s as 'still agreeable' although it 'has lost much of its old-fashioned rusticity and seclusion since the opening of the railways'. It lost even more in the course of the next century, although not everything: the George Inn, which claims to go back to the reign of King Charles II, still stands in the High Street, and there are other Georgian survivals.

Bromley, which gives its name to the London borough of which Beckenham today forms a part, also retains something of the appearance of the old market town it once was. Since the market continues, in some sense it still is, though the Victorian High Street, including the birthplace of H. G. Wells, was largely rebuilt between the wars and there has been much reconstruction more recently. Old private estates such as Shortlands were divided up into building plots over one hundred years ago.

In some ways Beckenham may be taken as a typical southeastern suburb, in which the effects of the succession of developments in settlement and transportation on what was always a fairly well-to-do sort of place can be traced since the 18th century.

**The George Inn,** *Beckenham*

In the early 19th century Beckenham was largely agricultural, with a population of about 2,000. There were a few old private estates, including Beckenham Place, the seat of the Lords of the manor, and a handful of more recent large houses, built for those who had made their pile in the City more recently. One of these served as Lord Mayor of London in 1839 and presumably commuted to the Mansion House in the Lord Mayor's Coach. There were also a fair number of people – about one third of the working population – who worked either in London or in Croydon.

Development was rapid from the 1850s. Beckenham itself did not get a railway station until 1857, but the London and Croydon (opened 1839) was

**Old house in Beckenham**, *c.* 1900. This quaint survival, photographed at the end of the 19th century, was known as Ye Olde Woode House. At that time it was occupied by three different shops, a sweet shop, laundry and jeweller, all apparently 'Ye Olde . . .' although one would have thought that was not a particularly attractive prefix for a laundry. The building survived more than one earlier attempt to have it pulled down before it finally succumbed in December 1920, amid some controversy. The site is now occupied by a boxy little house and shop, at present Ye Olde W. H. Smith.

not far away. For some time Beckenham had a number of residents of a rougher aspect than it has generally been accustomed to – 200 navvies engaged in rebuilding the Crystal Palace. It also had three gas street lamps in the 1850s and in 1869, it would seem, a minor labour shortage, since sheep were admitted to the churchyard to keep the grass down.

The various changes in local government which took place during the last thirty years of the 19th century caused a certain amount of dislocation. Under the act of 1894 Beckenham was large enough to be classed as an 'urban district'. The population was then approaching 25,000, and most of the old estates had disappeared to make room for surburban housing (a few mansions survived, including Beckenham Place, now the golf clubhouse). Road improvement had done away with the village stocks and the trees on Church Hill had been felled to make room for a police station. Electric street lights were installed in 1901.

The old village was dead; it was not possible to say exactly when it had died, though it's difficult to think of an 'urban district' as a village in any circumstances. As in so many other places, what was most to be regretted in its passing was not so much the changed appearance of the place but the loss of its spirit of community. A local historian, writing in 1910, lamented the declining interest in local affairs: 'We doubt whether there is the same keen interest in the election of the members of the district council as there used to be in the day of the Vestry'.

Since then the population has continued to grow, and houses and roads to increase. Love Lane has become a busy thoroughfare. Not many miles south of here in the 1820s, William Cobbett, riding through woods now bisected by the M25, had remarked that for over a mile the lane was completely arched over by branches. 'What an odd taste that man must have,' he remarked, 'who prefers a turnpike-road to a lane like this!'

In the housing boom of the interwar period there was little space left in Beckenham to accommodate speculative building, and the builders moved on to West Wickham. Beckenham became a municipal borough in 1935, shortly after completion of the town hall, and in 1965 was absorbed by the Greater London borough of Bromley.

## Varied patterns

If Beckenham may be taken as characteristic of the surburbs of the southeast, that is not to say that other places followed a similar pattern. Some did, some did not. Croydon, for example, was, like Kingston-upon-Thames, too big a place to be suburbanised, and the highly ambitious restructuring of the town in recent years demonstrates its uncompromisingly urban character. At the other extreme, a place such as Orpington, in spite of considerable building on what were once market gardens, is far enough away from the Great Wen to have very largely retained the rural character for which it has long been admired. Indeed, one Victorian guidebook felt compelled to state that some of the cottages and houses in Orpington were new, 'showing that the place is not merely a relic of the past, but making progress'. In the Victorian view, you could be as picturesque as you liked, but not if 'progress' were thereby inhibited. Perhaps that notions has not changed much – consider the Channel Tunnel rail link.

**Coulsdon**, The Brighton Road, 1906. As its condition shows, was still used almost exclusively by horses. Within a year or two, however, it had been resurfaced for the convenience of rubber-tyred motor vehicles. The Brighton Road is, along with the Dover Road and the Great North Road, one of the most romantic thoroughfares leading to and from London. Its most splendid period, no doubt, was the decade or so immeciately before the railway was built, when Brighton was at its most fashionable and horse-drawn carriages and coaches were at their peak.

**Camberwell,** *c.* 1950. By the 1950s the former village of Camerwell (an old spelling) or Camberwell, after which the butterfly was named, had long assumed the character of a middle-zone London suburb. The fair once held on Camberwell Green was not even a memory, having been ended a century earlier, at about the same time as the ancient church of St Giles burned down (the replacement by Gilbert Scott contains some stained glass designed by John Ruskin, a local resident whose name is commemorated in Ruskin Park).

The old borough of Camberwell included Peckham and Dulwich, but in the reorganization of 1965 Camberwell became part of the Greater London borough of Southwark. This scene has not changed fundamentally in the past generation. Lyons Tea Shop is, unfortunately, but a fond memory, and the tramlines were even then on the point of disappearing.

**Lewisham,** *c.* 1950. The tower blocks had not yet arrived though the basic layout is the same today. King James I is said to have been so impressed by the length of the High Street that he remarked he 'would be king of Lewisham'. It was then a street of farms and large mansions, and Lewisham remained a fashionable, rich suburb until the mid-19th century when the railways brought it within reach of a large number. By about 1900 the farmhouses and mansions had all disappeared from the High Street to be replaced by shops, and new streets and terraces spread over the fields and parkland. However, there was little industrial development until the 20th century and Lewisham was still, though undoubtedly a suburb, a middle-class one. The clock tower (centre) was erected in about 1900 and commemorates Queen Victoria's Diamond Jubilee and the achievement of metropolitan borough status.

*Camberwell c. 1950*

*Lewisham c. 1950*

*Forest Hill* c. 1900

**Forest Hill,** c. 1900. This is Devonshire Road, now a busy link with the South Circular, at about the turn of the century. The station is out of sight to the right.

The old meat market has been cut back and fronted by public lavatories. The pavement west of David's Road was raised for the better protection of pedestrians and St John's Presbyterian Church has gone, demolished in 1982. The modern street lamps are more efficient though less attractive.

The district has changed a good deal in this century and the Victorian houses have been disappearing fast, to be replaced by blocks of flats (one is visible now on the horizon). However, this section of Devonshire Road has changed remarkably little.

*Forest Hill* today

**Dulwich,** College Road, *c.* 1898. It says a lot for the determination of Dulwich to surrender as little of its past as possible that the old tollgate in College Road was still present and functioning in 1989, the last one in Greater London. The toll is not large, and for livestock it is still only 2½d (old pence), but no one has driven his sheep that way for some time. As tollgates go, this one is not especially ancient, having been erected in 1789 by a farmer who rented his land from Dulwich College and must have thought it worth his while to charge the travellers proceeding on the track from Dulwich towards Sydenham. Over one hundred tolls on public roads in London were removed in 1864 and a special act of parliament ended them altogether in 1871: most of them had become uneconomical due to railway competition. However, College Road is a private road and the tollgate, besides having picturesque appeal, is supposed to serve the useful purpose of discouraging drivers from using the road as a short cut to Sydenham. It operates only during the day, being left open at night.

**College Road Tollgate** today

**Dulwich College** c 1898

*College Road Tollgate* c. 1898

**Crystal Palace,** c 1890. The Crystal Palace, the plan for which was submitted by Joseph Paxton for the Great Exhibition of 1851, the first international exhibition ever held in England, was surely one of the 19th-century wonders of the world, although the reason Paxton's plan was chosen was not unconnected with the fact that it was miles the cheapest. In the words of a modern architectural historian, it was 'truly epoch-making, not only because this was the most direct and rational solution to a particular problem but also because the detailing of this 1,800-foot-long building was designed in such a way that all its parts could be factory-made and assembled on the site – the first ever example of prefabrication.'

This feature made it possible, when the Exhibition was over, to take the whole thing apart – 4,000 tons of iron, 400 tons of glass and 200 miles of wooden sash bars – and re-erect it on the high ground south-west of Sydenham. In fact, the building at Sydenham was not identical. It was larger than the Hyde Park version, and

among the new features were the 282-foot towers (one visible on the right), which enclose chimneys. They were designed by I. K. Brunel.

The palace was set on grand terraces, some remnants of which are still there along with the plaster dinosaurs, and among extensive pleasure gardens. The whole site occupied about 200 acres. It was a favourite resort of middle and lower-middle class families, providing accommodation for exhibitions, concerts, plays, as well as a restaurant and a zoo (an elephant called Charlie once escaped and caused some havoc in the gardens before being recaptured). The F.A. Cup Final was played here before Wembley Stadium was built. Today the park contains other splendid sporting facilities, including a sports hall, swimming pool, ski slope and stadium.

The palace itself stood for over 80 years, and it was a national disaster when fire finally destroyed the whole magnificent edifice in 1936. Brunel's water towers survived the fire but were demolished a few years later.

**Crystal Palace** c. 1890

*Streatham High Road, c. 1950*

**Streatham High Road,** *c.* 1950 and the same view today. The buildings have not changed much, and the scene is still dominated by St Leonard's Church. Indeed, the church was there centuries before any of these buildings existed, though it was almost completely rebuilt in the 1830s.

This is still a busy shopping street, but Pratt's department store (the name is visible above the clock) has migrated to the other side of the road (and out of sight), while still retaining the upper floors of the building which houses one of the ubiquitous Macdonalds hamburger restaurants. The rise of fast food shops has been a notable feature of the changing English High Street since the Second World War.

*The same view today*

**Upper Norwood,** *c.* 1900. One of Brunel's Crystal Palace water towers is trailing a plume of smoke which makes it look as if it is about to come steaming down Westow Hill in Upper Norwood. The photograph was taken soon after the turn of the century, when plum jam could be had for 7½d (3p) a pound.

Upper Norwood, which owes its name to the Great North Wood which covered a large stretch of what is now south London, was already a prosperous little suburb in Regency times. It was transformed by the arrival of the Crystal Palace – and the accommodating railways – and was rapidly built up with homes, mainly large ones, shops and inns. As its fortunes rose with the Palace, though, so did they decline. Between the wars, when Crystal Palace was declining in popularity and finally ended in the great blaze of 1936, Upper Norwood became somewhat neglected. It has never quite recovered its former smartness, although the National Sports Centre at Crystal Palace has given it a new focus.

**Bromley Park**, Shortlands, *c.* 1900. The Ravensbourne River is visible in the background. Shortlands was named after the 18th-century Shortlands House (now a Roman Catholic school). The grounds of Shortlands House were sold for building plots in the 1860s, soon after the arrival of the railway, whereupon Shortlands developed rapidly into a suburb. However, there is still plenty of open space.

**Bromley High St,** 1899 and today. The cranes are out but they are not pulling down the splendidly chateauesque Aberdeen Buildings (1887) which have had a preservation order placed on them. Otherwise, practically nothing remains of the High Street of 1899. The Methodist Church has been demolished, and much of the buildings in the area beyond it are coming down in preparation for a new shopping precinct. More has changed in Bromley during the past 150 years than in the previous thousand years when it was a manor of the Bishop of Rochester.

***Upper Norwood*** *c. 1900*

***Bromley Park*** *c. 1900*

**Bromley High Street** 1899

**Bromley High Street** today

**Croydon, The Swan and Sugar Loaf** c. 1905 ·

**The same view today**

**Croydon**, The Swan & Sugar Loaf, *c.* 1905. This splendid Victorian pub (the date on the gable is 1896) stands at what was and is a major crossroads in Croydon, where South End becomes the Brighton Road (not far from South Croydon railway station). The tram is bound from Thornton Heath to Purley, the horse bus for Brixton station.

Croydon was the largest town in Surrey before it became a Greater London borough in 1965, and can scarcely be regarded as a suburb; one hundred years ago it had no less than eight railway stations (including Thornton Heath and Addiscombe but excluding the central station in Katharine Street which was already out of commission).

But Croydon has always been a place for keeping up with the times. Before the end of the 19th century the Corporation organised redevelopment of the Middle Row area, a notorious slum. Bombs caused much destruction during the Second World War and from about 1960 a positively Dallas-like redevelopment took place in central Croydon, described in the current Blue Guide as 'the most thoroughgoing Civic rebuilding undertaken since 1945 in England'.

**Croydon Airport Hotel**

**Croydon Airport,** *c.* 1930. Croydon airport was opened in 1915, and was originally a military institution, charged with the defence of London. In 1920, on the closure of Hounslow, Croydon became the London Customs Air Port, the chief civil aerodrome for the capital. Following the recommendations of the Civil Aviation Board, improvements and extensions were made and it reopened as the official Airport of London in 1928. So it remained until after the Second World War, when Heathrow was constructed. The Croydon Airport of London was finally closed in 1959, after the opening of Gatwick a few miles to the south, which made Croydon redundant. The main administrative block s now a hotel.

***Croydon Airport,*** *c. 1930*

**Croydon North End** 1896

**Croydon North End,** 1896. The centre of Croydon has been transformed in the present generation. Although none of the buildings visible here is of any outstanding merit in itself, in total the view is rather more impressive, and much the same could be said of contemporary Croydon, where the strength of commitment to urban regeneration is very striking.

**Caterham**, *c.* 1903. Around Caterham, wrote John Aubrey, were 'many pleasant valleys, stored with wild thyme, marjoram, burnet, boscage and beeches'. James Thorne, a century later, remarked that Caterham village, 'though "improved" still retains an air of old-fashioned picturesqueness' and he considered that 'the whole neighbourhood remains perhaps the pleasantest of those near London which have been made the prey of the railway engineer, speculative builder, and . . . build ng societies.' The population then was 3,577 'or, excluding the inmates of the Asylum for imbeciles, 2,250' (the institution is now known as St Lawrence's Hospital and the building is scheduled for demolition in 1990).

Buildings and population have increased considerably in the 20th century, but without destroying the character of the place. There are still 'boscy valleys and thymey downs' around Caterham: Timber Hill, seen below in 1903, is in the middle of the town. It was

**The White Lion** today

presented to the town by a member of a well-known firm of London jewellers who lived in Caterham towards the end of the 19th century and it is now a recreation ground.

**Warlingham**, The White Lion, *c.* 1905 and today. It is interesting to note the phoney half-timbering introduced to make the inn seem even more venerable than it is. Otherwise, apart from the new houses in the background, the view has changed little; even the flint wall at the left has survived, though the carriage house beyond the pub has been converted.

Warlington was described in the late Victorian period as 'a few humble cottages gathered about a broad Green, two or three sleepy shops, a smithy, a Methodist chapel, and a couple of little inns, the Leather Bottle and the White Lion – the latter also a general shop – with a farm-house or two . . .'

Though much enlarged in recent times, it is still a pleasantly rural place amid the downs. Farms bearing odd names like 'Halliloo' and 'Batts' are still at work, and nearby is the tranquil development of Woldingham Garden Village.

**Caterham,** *Timber Hill c. 1903*

**Warlingham,** *The White Lion c. 1905*

# THE SOUTH WEST:
## TO THE BRIGHTON ROAD
# CHAPTER EIGHT

Although on the whole people tend to express a preference for the area in which they happen to live themselves (and what a good thing!), probably the most popular suburban segment of Greater London and beyond is the southwest, between the Brighton Road and the Bath Road or, as modern motorists might say, between the M23 and the M4. This is partly due to the proximity of the River Thames, which winds its placid way through this sector (see Chapter 4), escorted by echelons of reservoirs – so many and so large that from the air you might suppose you were over the Lake District or the Norfolk Broads. It is due also to the proximity of fine countryside (it is now possible to commute from Dorset, though some would say it ought to be forbidden) and to good transportation (generally superior to the southeast, especially if you travel a lot by air), partly perhaps even to the tiny but real difference in climate (warmer than the north, drier than the southeast), and partly to historical reasons, hard to gauge, such as the effect on the environment of a relatively high density of noble mansions and palaces.

### Sporting life

Among the attractions of the southwest suburbs several are connected with sporting occupations. The number of race courses in this small area is remarkably high. Kempton Park, Sandown and Epsom are all within a few miles of each other; Windsor and Ascot (perhaps more famous for the ostentatious clothes of the wealthy than the high quality of the racing) are not far away. There are some famous golf courses and of course there are the national headquarters, one might almost say international shrines, of two of the most popular games, at Wimbledon (tennis) and at Twickenham (rugby union), as well as, among others, the National Rifle Association at Bisley and the place of origin (or one of them) of field hockey, at Teddington.

The Wimbledon lawn tennis championship is arguably the most famous sporting occasion in the world. Its popularity has been hugely increased during the past twenty years by television, and, contrary to the fears of many sporting administrators, the excellence of the television coverage, so far from discouraging attendance in the flesh, seems to have had the opposite effect. Tickets sell at such huge prices on the black market now that corruption scandals involving officials and others entitled to tickets have been aired in the newspapers.

The village of Wimbledon grew up around Wimbledon House, at one time the property of the Cecils, then of the Spencers. Some early buildings still survive in the High Street, among them Eagle House (once the home of Lord

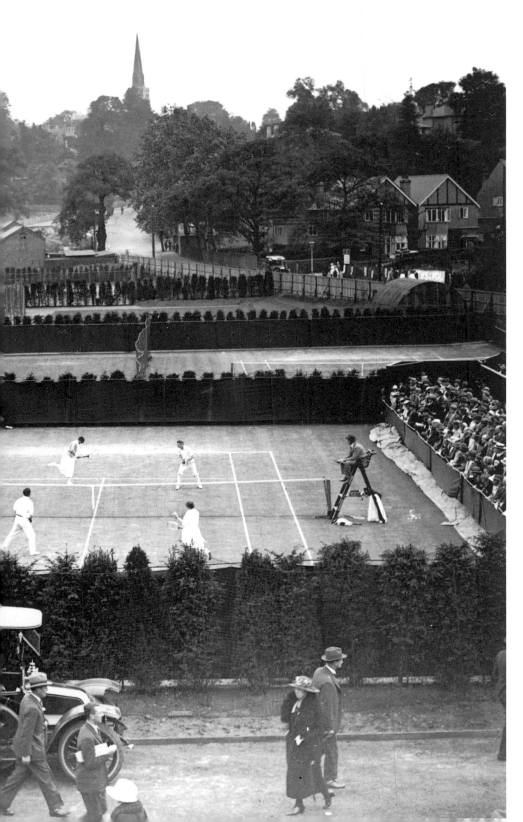

Grenville, Pitt's cousin and political associate, later a school, now offices) and the 17th-century Rose and Crown. Otherwise, Wimbledon, which had a railway station in 1838, was mightily redeveloped in Victorian times, and because the station had to be built at some distance from the old village (the original station building has now become the Railway Tavern), Wimbledon spread over a wide area. Wimbledon Common fortunately survived the intense speculative building, and today adds to the attraction of the place as a commuter's suburb, fifteen minutes from Waterloo.

## Tennis

Lawn tennis was invented, like so many games, by a bored British army officer, a Major Wingfield, who was granted a patent in 1874 for something he called (having had a classical education) sphairistiké, modelled on the ancient game of 'real' tennis. Renamed and simplified, lawn tennis became a popular pastime in the large gardens of the late Victorian middle class. Rules were published by the Marylebone Cricket Club, the ruling body of cricket, but the game was also taken up by the All-England Croquet Club, hitherto enjoying a monopoly of those aforementioned lawns, whose headquarters were in Wimbledon (Worple Road in those days). The first Wimbledon tennis championship was held as early as 1878, before Dan Maskell was born, and since then Wimbledon tennis has become steadily more popular.

Croquet beat a hasty retreat to Hurlingham, but the Wimbledon organization is still called the All England Lawn Tennis and Croquet Club. It has been in its present quarters at Church Road since 1922, though the premises have been much expanded and improved since then. At present over 30,000 spectators can be accommodated, nearly half of them around the Centre Court. The grass courts are used only during the annual championship; there are clay courts for play at other times. Wimbledon has become the last major tennis tournament to be played on grass courts.

**Wimbledon Tennis Courts** *c.* 1923. The world's greatest tennis championships have always been held on the courts of the All-England Club at Wimbledon, a place now familiar to millions throughout the world thanks to the popularity of the occasion on television. The first men's championships were held as early as 1877, when the players wore collars and ties and the balls were plain rubber – no cloth. The headquarters of the Club (originally the All-England Croquet Club) were off Worple Road; it moved to its present site in 1922. There have been continuous changes, improvements and extensions ever since.

## Rugby football

Games that were not thought up by idle British officers often seem to have been created by inventive British public-school boys (or in the case of cricket, by idle and inventive Hampshire shepherds); though the theory of the cack-footed lad Ellis at Rugby School picking up the ball during a game of 'footer', and thus setting in train events leading to the game now played at Twickenham Rugby Ground, seems rather unlikely even for a sporting tale.

The present headquarters of the Rugby Football Union, just west of Twickenham, were bought by William Williams in 1907 and for a time known as 'Billy Williams's Cabbage Patch' (the name lives on in a nearby pub). The premises, England's home ground since 1908, have been expanded considerably over the years, both in area (the original car park held two hundred cars which considering the scarcity of motor vehicles in 1908 could be said to show striking forethought, however laughably inadequate it seems now) and in volume. The latest addition to the latter is the cantilevered South Stand, opened in 1981. The total capacity of the ground (including standing spectators) is about 62,000, less than it used to be in fact, although a higher proportion is now seated. The grounds of roughly half the most distinguished rugby football clubs in Greater London

(Harlequins, Richmond, London Welsh, London Scottish, and so on) are within a mile or two of Twickenham.

Suburban development in the southwest, until the booming 1920s, was less intense than it was, for instance, in Metroland. Beyond Wandsworth housing density tended to be lower than in other comparable districts, which encouraged the idea (probably correct) that the population of this area was on average wealthier. But there were some surprising variations in residential growth throughout Surrey north of the downs. For example, Sutton was a well-established suburb in mid-Victorian times, but Cheam, the neighbour which goes with Sutton as familiarly as Laurel with Hardy, remained essentially a country village until after the First World War. Places such as West Drayton or Harmondsworth were transformed by the coming of the airport to Heathrow, with the accompanying demand for houses, roads and ancillary buildings in the immediate neighborhood.

## Leatherhead

Leatherhead itself is a town which has changed more in size than in character during the past one hundred years, having been described a century ago as 'a very quiet place'. The same account complained that 'the picturesqueness of the place as a whole, formerly very marked, has been almost improved away of late years.' Old prints reveal, however, that a certain amount of smartening up was called for if Leatherhead were to fulfil its divinely appointed role as a dormitory town for the prosperous middle class. Otherwise, changes have been mainly cosmetic and concerned with traffic movement. The Bull Inn, the parish church and the red-brick pile of St John's School were all present a century ago.

Traffic has been and is a different problem for all these small Surrey towns. Leatherhead was one of the first to have a bypass, which is now linked with the M25, running just north of the town, but this has not turned the streets of Leatherhead into a haven of peace and tranquillity. In some respects the M25 has generated more problems than it solved, especially in attracting greater volumes of traffic than were estimated. Motorways (which were forecast, incidentally, by H. G. Wells in 1900) came late to Britain, yet the traffic problems we endured before they were built do not now, less than thirty years since the construction of the M1, seem in retrospect as bad as those of today.

There is still plenty of open country north of Leatherhead, as there is – although of a more thoroughly domesticated sort – again to the north and west of Kingston-upon-Thames. In between, however, lies a great swathe of surburbia stretching from Wandsworth to Sutton.

***Twickenham Rugby Ground*** *c. 1908*

## Sutton

Sutton ('southern farmstead') itself, which traces its existence to early Saxon times, remained a farming village for a thousand years or so, first coming into prominence with the building of the turnpike road from London to Brighton in the mid-18th century. It then acquired several famous inns, but it did not begin to grow appreciably until after the continuation of the railway line to Epsom in 1847 and a further connection with the South Western at Wimbledon in 1868. Sutton then became a dormitory town, and the Victorian new town was built to the north of the old village, with another famous inn, the Jenny Lind (a popular name for pubs around that time after the great success of 'the Swedish nightingale'), and a new church, All Saints.

Sutton continued to expand during the present century, although the plan to continue the District Line from Wimbledon to Sutton has not yet been put into effect (and presumably never will be). In 1928 Sutton was incorporated as a municipal borough with Cheam, but unlike Sutton, Cheam was not seriously developed until the 1920s and retains rather more of its older village buildings, including the 16th-century half-timbered house of Whitehall, once occupied by Cheam School and, after restoration, opened to the public in 1978. As in other north Surrey boroughs, there has been little or no industrial development to jeopardise the residential calm.

Much as Cheam became amalgamated with Sutton, and Ewell with Epsom, the ancient borough of Kingston has absorbed the settlements to the south and east. Norbiton ('north tun', as distant from Surbiton, 'south tun')

**The Greyhound,** Sutton High Street 1932. A resident of Sutton in the first decade of the 20th century who returned to the town today would probably not find the old place very familiar. He or she would, for a start, be bewildered by the one-way traffic system, which seems to be in a permanent state of flux, and the whole atmosphere of the place would seem entirely different. And yet, large areas of the centre of Sutton have remained virtually untouched by the eager hands of 20th-century developers since the days of the horse and cart. W. J. Bowling, the all-purpose hardware merchant ('wholesale and furnishing, ironmonger, plumber, gas and hot water fitter', among other useful attributes), may have been replaced by the Midland Bank, but the building is the same.

On the whole inns have survived the ravages of progress pretty well, if one ignores the inevitable reconstruction. There are probably as many old inns left around London as there are old churches.

and New Malden were built up from the late 19th century. The latter, largely occupying what had been Norbiton Common, had a particularly good reputation in the 19th century, earning the nickname, 'the Montpelier of Surrey', absurdly enough, and there was some dissension among the inhabitants when it was made part of the Greater London borough of Kingston in 1965, although, as it happened, before the mid-19th century New Malden had been part of Kingston parish.

**Mitcham,** *Fair Green c. 1960*

## Mitcham

There are more old inns to the east in Mitcham, another old settlement, said to have originated as a defensive settlement made to guard south London in the 5th century. It was a fashionable place in Elizabethan times, when a number of courtiers had houses here. The Buck's Head Inn is named after the family crest of one of them; the building is modern, however. Two other Mitcham inns, the White Hart and the Burn Bullock, probably go back to the reign of Elizabeth, although the present buildings date from the period after the construction of the turnpike road in 1745. There are several old houses too, notably Eagle House, Canons and Park Place. In the 19th century Mitcham was known for its production of medicinal and cosmetic herbs, but the chemical industry, the railway and the cost of land combined to turn the old village into the modern suburb, though the process was not completed until recent times. Old customs continue, including the fair thought to have been chartered in the 16th century, and the cricket club, which claims to have been founded in 1707 although cricketing historians, especially those of Hampshire origin, regard this as improbable.

## Raynes Park

Raynes Park, in the borough of Merton, is largely a railway creation. The 'park', which belonged to Mr Rayne, was sold to the South Western Railway in 1855 for construction of the line to Woking, and the parish grew up around the new railway station. Worcester Park was originally part of the park belonging to the Tudor palace of Nonsuch, and takes its name from an earl of Worcester who was keeper of the park in the 17th century. At Worcester Park farm house, which still survives, Holman Hunt painted his famous picture *The Light of the World* (one version of which is in St Paul's Cathedral) with his fellow Pre-Raphaelite, Millais, as the model for Jesus. At that time suburban development had begun, following the construction of the railway to Leatherhead, when a station was located at Worcester Park, but the area was not really built up until the interwar period, and there has been further development since 1945.

Morden was similarly a late developer. An ancient place, with Romano-British remains and references in Saxon charters, it was crossed by the Roman road called Stane Street, which now runs several feet below the surface of Morden Park. Morden Hill, a 17th-century house considerably altered in early Victorian times, now belongs to the National Trust, and among other old buildings the George Inn is said to date from the 16th century. Morden was still a genuine village after the First World War, until the building of the Northern Line terminus in 1926.

**Mitcham,** Fair Green, c. 1960. The Buck's Head Inn (the sign is just visible to the left of the large tree) is named after the family crest of the Smythe family, who lived here in the 16th century. The present inn dates from the turn of the century, but two other inns, the Burn Bullock and the White Hart, date from the building of the Turnpike in 1745. Queen Elizabeth I visited fashionable Mitcham on more than one occasion, and when Sir Julius Caesar (later Master of the Rolls) was her host, the poor man afterwards lamented that her 24-hour visit had cost him over £700, a truly colossal sum for those days. Sir Walter Raleigh also had a house in Mitcham.

As late as 1911 Mitcham was described as a neighbourhood abounding in 'market gardens and plantations of aromatic herbs for the manufacture of scents and essences', though the business was by then contracting fast. Forty years earlier, it was said, 'roses, lavender and peppermint . . . and liquorice, aniseed, poppies, mint, chamomiles, and other medicinal plants cover hundreds of acres, and perfume the air for a considerable distance'.

The fair which used to be held on the Fair Green (or Upper Green, as distinguished from the equally celebrated Lower, or Cricket, Green) was moved to a new, less inconvenient situation in 1928. Records of the fair exist from the early 18th century but it was probably in existence much earlier. The unusually rich and interesting history of the village contains similar mysteries, such as that shrouding the early years of Mitcham cricket club.

**Wimbledon Hill Road**, *c.* 1954. It is strange how little things can get such a grip on the environment: in photographs of urban scenes taken up to about this time, the eye registers the blessed absence of the mad spiders web of television aerials on the rooftops (satellite 'dishes' will be worse) and of the thick, double, puke-yellow bands lining the streets in a vain attempt to warn off cars. It is true that neither of these features can seriously be said to blight the beauty of Wimbledon, but in places built on a smaller architectural scale they can be wantonly intrusive.

**Wimbledon Hill Road** today

**Wimbledon High Street** *c.* 1920. Wimbledon first grew at the top of the hill, around Wimbledon House (destroyed long ago) which was built on land granted to Sir Thomas Cecil by Queen Elizabeth. The church, and such as there are of pre-Industrial Revolution remains in Wimbledon, are to be found in the old High Street which is part of the mediaeval village. Two of the original seventeenth century buildings still standing are Eagle House and the Rose and Crown (see right). When the railway station was built half a mile away at the bottom of the hill, Wimbledon Hill Road (see left) — and numerous adjacent residential streets — were rapidly built up. The Railway Tavern was once the original railway station.

*Wimbledon High Street c. 1920*

*Wimbledon High Street today*

**Wimbledon Common** today (overleaf). The Common is actually the remains of waste land belonging to the Manor of Wimbledon which was too poor for cultivation. There has been a windmill on the site at least since 1613, but the original one had disappeared by the end of the 18th century. By 1816 a new one was being built, and this ground corn for the surrounding districts until 1864. The Lord of the Manor, Earl Spencer, then attempted to enclose the Common, and converted the mill into six cottages. His attempts were defeated by Sir Henry Peake, M.P. and resulted in the Wimbledon and Putney Commons Act of 1871 which guaranteed their preservation. The mill, which was subsequently repaired and restored is now a museum.

**Sutton High Street** *c. 1900*

**Sutton High Street** *today*

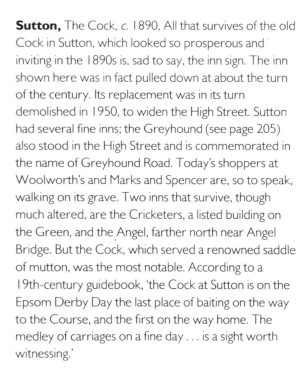

**Sutton,** The Cock, *c.* 1890, All that survives of the old Cock in Sutton, which looked so prosperous and inviting in the 1890s is, sad to say, the inn sign. The inn shown here was in fact pulled down at about the turn of the century. Its replacement was in its turn demolished in 1950, to widen the High Street. Sutton had several fine inns; the Greyhound (see page 205) also stood in the High Street and is commemorated in the name of Greyhound Road. Today's shoppers at Woolworth's and Marks and Spencer are, so to speak, walking on its grave. Two inns that survive, though much altered, are the Cricketers, a listed building on the Green, and the Angel, farther north near Angel Bridge. But the Cock, which served a renowned saddle of mutton, was the most notable. According to a 19th-century guidebook, 'the Cock at Sutton is on the Epsom Derby Day the last place of baiting on the way to the Course, and the first on the way home. The medley of carriages on a fine day . . . is a sight worth witnessing.'

*Sutton, **The Cock,** c. 1890*

**Malden,** St John's Church, c. 1900. The church was described by John Thorne, the somewhat brusque author of the Victorian guide to the Greater London area, as 'small, of no interest, and contains no monuments' (the Victorians were very keen on monuments). No doubt the church, whose brick tower dates from a Jacobean reconstruction, is no great architectural gem, but today a large part of Malden Manor, including the church, is a conservation area. The church is approached through trees, whose growth makes it impossible to duplicate precisely the view of about the beginning of the century with the view today.

Malden Manor was listed in Domesday Book. In the 13th century it belonged to Walter de Merton. He established a small religious house here which became incorporated with Merton College, Oxford, subsequently proprietors of the manor.

New Malden is naturally a more recent development. According to the local historian F. Somner Merryweather, writing in the 1880s, the rise of the village in the valley was not altogether pleasing to the older inhabitants, and they were able to use their influence to ensure that New Malden station, the occasion for the development, offered a rather poor service, with few trains actually stopping there. Nevertheless, property prices boomed. The quarter-acre of land required for building the police station cost £500.

Left: *St John's Church, Malden* c. 1900. **Above:** *the same view today*

**Wallington,** Manor Road, *c.* 1903 (right). The Melbourne tavern is still on the corner though it has been rebuilt to look more Victorian than it did in Victorian times, a squat postwar office block has obtruded on the scene farther down the road, and the houses beyond the pub have been renovated, losing their chimney stacks and gaining burglar alarms.

Wallington, a sister village of Beddington and Carshalton, was also associated with the herb-growing business of this area which was centred on Mitcham. The railway station, which stood in open fields until quite late in the 19th century, was originally called Carshalton station. Wallington was also served by what is claimed to be the first public railway in the world, the Surrey Iron Railway, a horse-driven railway (you had to provide your own horse) which ran from Wandsworth via Merton and Mitcham to Croydon, with a branch line to Carshalton, at the beginning of the 19th century.

**Carshalton,** *c.* 1896 and the same view today. Carshalton ponds, which form one course of the River Wandle, have had a marked effect on the history of the village. They have made life difficult for through traffic and thus helped to preserve the character of the place: the centre of Carshalton is today a conservation area. Nevertheless, the main road has become very busy: this photograph was taken early on a Sunday morning (though not quite early enough to catch the effect of the rising sun shining through the windows of All Saints Church).

The 18th-century house known as Queen's Well was demolished about thirty years ago. In its place is a residential home for the elderly, sensitively designed to blend in with the environment. Part of the old Greyhound Inn is visible on the right in today's photograph.

*Carshalton c. 1896*

**Wallington,** *Manor Road c. 1903*

**Cheam** today

**Cheam,** Station Way, 1904. Although the railway came to Cheam before 1850, the village did not begin to develop into a prosperous suburb, containing many large, detached houses, until after the First World War. It was described as still essentially a Surrey farming village in the 1920s.

The two views here are separated in time by over eighty years. During that period most of Cheam's modern development took place, yet there is no significant change here. The large late Victorian house in the background has now been almost completely obscured by the enlarged railway bridge, and the railway building on the left has been enthusiastically renovated. In fact there have been rather more dramatic changes in the immediate area that are visible in this photograph.

**Cheam,** Station Way 1904

**Esher,** the River Mole c. 1950

***The River Mole*** *today*

**Esher,** the River Mole, *c.* 1950 The River Mole is one
of the attractions of surburban Surrey. It rises near
Horsham in Sussex and flows through Surrey, breaking
through the North Downs near Dorking, living up to its
name as a subterranean burrower for a while in the
chalk between Dorking and Leatherhead, and
eventually reaches the Thames at East Molesey
(meaning 'Mole island'). West of Esher it winds a
tortuous way through water meadows where the
landscape is still green and open (and the river is still
liable to flood after heavy rains, though less so than in
Victorian times).

**Epsom,** Derby Day, c. 1930. This occasion has been described as 'one of the last real folk festivals'. Traditionally there has always been a conflict between the profit makers and the regular users of the Downs, and the actual horse-race is merely the excuse for numerous other activities.

Although racing on the Downs probably predates the discovery of the mineral wells, it was the latter which made the racing so popular, though in the early years it was racing of a highly informal kind. The grandstand shown here was built in 1927, after the old grandstand, which was then nearly a century old, had been demolished. Various additions (such as the Rosebery Stand, 1960) have been made since.

***Epsom High Street*** *today*

***Epsom,*** *Derby Day c. 1930*

**Epsom High Street,** c. 1897. Like most other old country towns with a distinguished past, Epsom has suffered widely at the hands of developers during the past hundred years. 'Numerous listed buildings have been pulled down over the past decade or so', complained a local historian, Brian J. Salter, in 1976, 'many by one particular "development" company, often after becoming beyond repair through systematic neglect'. Epsom is certainly an example of how meaningless the classification of 'conservation area' can be. The once celebrated mineral springs, discovered in 1618 and from which Epsom salts were first extracted, are now no longer used.

Waterloo House, on the right in these photographs, is a notable survivor. It dates from 1690 and although at one time a tavern it served as assembly rooms in the days when Epsom was a popular spa. In the 19th century cockfights were held here, and the building has gone through a variety of humbling experiences, culminating in the restoration of 1962 when for some reason the horrid ground-floor frontage was retained.

The familiar clock tower is an early Victorian adornment, erected in 1854 on the site of a village pond which was filled in at that time by the newly created Local Board of Health.

**Epsom High Street** c. 1897

# INDEX

## Acknowledgements

With the exception of those from the following sources, the historical photographs in this book are from The Francis Frith Collection, Andover, and the modern ones were taken specially for the Octopus Group by Nick Wright.

Bexley Local Studies Service 22-3; The Bridgeman Art Library, London 11 (Kenwood House), 12-13 (Museum of London), 14 (Fishmongers' Hall), 17 (Roy Miles Fine Paintings), 18 (private collection); Britain on View Photographic Library (BTA/ETB) 73; London Borough of Ealing Local History Library 131 left; Mary Evans Picture Library, London 27, 48, 58-9, 68 right, 69 left, 70-1, 166-7 (Bruce Castle Museum); Greater London Photographic Library 85, 135 bottom, 165; Greenwich Local History Library 93, 98 (R. Westwood), 99 top; Guildhall Library, City of London 29, 61, 89, 182, 192-3; Hammersmith and Fulham Archives 107; Highgate Literary and Scientific Institution 144, 145; The Hulton-Deutsch Collection, London 30, 37, 202-3; A. F. Kersting 20, 77; London Transport Museum 26, 132, 134; from the Collections of Merton Library Service 209 top; Museum in Docklands Project 83, 84, 94-5; Museum of London 8, 9, 133, 164 bottom; Octopus Group Limited/Jonathan Potter 6-7, 10; Royal Commission on the Historical Monuments of England 42 left, 44, 64-5, 75; Rugby Football Union, Twickenham 204; Robert Smith 168 top; London Borough of Sutton Heritage Service 196 bottom, 197 left; Tower Hamlets Local History Library and Archives 96, 156, 164 top.

| | | | |
|---|---|---|---|
| Commissioning Editor | Trevor Dolby | Designers | Sarah Pollock |
| Editor | Alexa Stace | | Dave Robinson |
| Art Director/Design | Alyson Kyles | Production Control | Susan Brown |
| | | Picture Research | Judy Todd |

Text set by Dorchester Typesetting Group Ltd in 10pt Cheltenham and 10pt Gill Sans

The Publishers would like to thank the following organisations for their help in the production of this book.

The Francis Frith Collection, Charleton Road, Andover, Hampshire, SP10 3LE. Copies of their photographs reproduced in this book, and thousands more from around the country, may be obtained from them at this address. Linhof Professional Sales, 56 Marchmont Street, London WC2 for the loan of the 6 × 17 camera used in the production of the aerial panorama shots. Airship Industries for allowing our intrepid photographer, Nick Wright, up in their aircraft to take the aerial panorama shots.